THE PSYCHOLOGY OF COUNSELLING

What is counselling and how can it help? Does counselling work? How is counselling different from talking to my family and friends about my problems?

The Psychology of Counselling explains the different approaches to therapy and how they are used in practice, giving information on what counselling can help with and what it cannot do. It looks at cognitive and behavioural therapies, psychoanalysis, and humanistic psychology, as well as exploring positive psychotherapy and the move away from a disease-based approach to counselling. It also reflects upon the broader landscape of therapeutic spaces and gives consideration to professional issues in counselling, such as ethics, supervision, and duty of care to clients.

At a time when mental health and psychological well-being are central subjects of conversation in modern society, The Psychology of Counselling sheds light on the therapeutic process, what it involves, and how it works, to help all those seeking assistance for relieving emotional or psychological issues and improving their psychological wellness.

Marie Percival is an academic, practitioner, and researcher. With over 15 years of experience teaching psychology and psychological therapies to undergraduate and postgraduate students at higher educational institutions and dealing with countless clients during this period, she has acquired extensive knowledge in this field.

The Psychology of Everything

People are fascinated by psychology and what makes humans tick. Why do we think and behave the way we do? We've all met armchair psychologists claiming to have the answers, and people that ask if psychologists can tell what they're thinking. The Psychology of Everything is a series of books which debunk the popular myths and pseudo-science surrounding some of life's biggest questions.

The series explores the hidden psychological factors that drive us, from our subconscious desires and aversions, to our natural social instincts. Absorbing, informative, and always intriguing, each book is written by an expert in the field, examining how research-based knowledge compares with popular wisdom, and showing how psychology can truly enrich our understanding of modern life.

Applying a psychological lens to an array of topics and contemporary concerns – from sex, to fashion, to conspiracy theories – The Psychology of Everything will make you look at everything in a new way.

Titles in the series:

The Psychology of Democracy
Darren G. Lilleker, Billur Aslan Ozgul

The Psychology of Counselling
Marie Percival

For further information about this series please visit www. routledgetextbooks.com/textbooks/thepsychologyofeverything/

THE
PSYCHOLOGY
OF COUNSELLING

MARIE PERCIVAL

Routledge
Taylor & Francis Group

LONDON AND NEW YORK

Cover image: © Getty Images

First published 2023
by Routledge
4 Park Square, Milton Park, Abingdon, Oxon OX14 4RN

and by Routledge
605 Third Avenue, New York, NY 10158

Routledge is an imprint of the Taylor & Francis Group, an informa business

British Library Cataloguing-in-Publication Data
A catalogue record for this book is available from the British Library

ISBN: 978-1-032-05185-7 (hbk)
ISBN: 978-1-032-05180-2 (pbk)
ISBN: 978-1-003-19647-1 (ebk)

DOI: 10.4324/9781003196471

Typeset in Joanna
by Apex CoVantage, LLC

In memory of my parents, Patrick and Monica McDowell

CONTENTS

Preface   ix
Acknowledgements   xv

1   Counselling – past, present and future   1

2   Freud psychoanalysis reviewed and reconsidered   17

3   Humanistic psychology – a person-centred
    approach to counselling   31

4   Cognitive behavioural therapy   45

5   The promise of positive psychology   61

6   The healing space – a changing landscape   77

7   Research in counselling and psychotherapy   91

8   Professional issues in counselling and psychotherapy   105

Further reading and web resources   121
References   125

PREFACE

Welcome to The Psychology of Counselling.

Counselling interests you, which is why you're reading this book. There may be a concern or issue that is causing you discomfort or distress and you have been advised to speak with someone about it. In most cases, the someone in question is a professional helper. Professional helpers use many names, such as counsellors, psychotherapists, therapists, or clinical psychologists, among others. This book provides a concise overview of the main approaches to counselling, making it suitable for those who are unfamiliar with, or considering seeking assistance from a counsellor. By knowing what counselling can help with and what it cannot do, the interested person will be able to manage their expectations when seeking professional help.

Additionally, students beginning their study programme or those considering a career in counselling will find The Psychology of Counselling to be of interest since it concludes with references to further reading and useful websites that will assist readers in gaining a deeper understanding of and knowledge of topics of interest.

CHAPTER OUTLINE

The first chapter of the book presents a brief history of counselling over time, from its origins in pastoral work and psychological influences to its current status as a professional discipline. This chapter aims to demystify the counselling process. There will be an explanation of what counselling is and what it is not, how therapy works, and how it may be effective for some people. This chapter reviews the literature on adverse childhood experiences, the buffering effects of positive experiences in the early years, and how these experiences impact mental health in adulthood. Chatbots and artificial intelligence (AI) are discussed in relation to the future of counselling and their role in providing emotional support.

Chapter 2 focuses on the work of Sigmund Freud, widely regarded to be the founding father of the talking cure. The influence Freud has on psychotherapy is undeniable, despite the contentious nature of his claims and rejection by colleagues within and outside the psychoanalytic community. We will review Freud's theories of human nature and outline the practice of psychoanalysis in this chapter. We will also reconsider Freud's theories in light of Mark Solms's work in, and argument for, neuropsychoanalysis. This controversial topic has been a source of much debate for the past two decades with some critics calling it anti-psychoanalytic.

Chapter 3 will introduce Carl Rogers's person-centred counselling. The key features of this humanistic approach will be described and an overview of person-centred counselling in practice will be summarised. The actualising tendency, which Rogers described as our innate motivation for growth and development will be explained. Rogers was resolute in his belief that our tendency towards growth could be thwarted or suppressed but never destroyed. His optimistic view of human nature will be discussed throughout the chapter. A description of the six necessary and sufficient conditions for therapy will be summarised. Rogers's view on the importance of love and acceptance in childhood and what it means to become a fully functioning person will be presented in this chapter.

Chapter 4 begins with a brief history of the development of CBT and an introduction to Aaron Beck and Albert Ellis. Throughout this chapter, the theory and practice of this problem-solving, highly structured, time-limited psychoeducational approach will be described. The influential role of thoughts in emotional and behavioural responses in psychological distress will be explained. This chapter will also consider developments in CBT, with an introduction to Acceptance and Commitment Therapy (ACT), Dialectical Behavioural Therapy and Recovery Oriented Cognitive therapy (CT-R).

Positive psychology, as defined by Martin Seligman, is discussed in Chapter 5. The PERMA wellbeing model, along with key features of positive psychotherapy, will be described, as well as the utility of adopting a strengths-based approach in therapy. In this chapter, we will introduce some positive psychology interventions (PPIs) and distinguish strengths-based positive psychotherapy from traditional pathology-focused therapy. Positive psychotherapy is often referred to as a move away from a 'what's wrong' to a 'what's strong' approach. This chapter will consider the utility of adopting a strengths-based approach to help people to develop meaningful relationships, live purposeful lives and enhance their wellbeing.

Due to the growing popularity of online counselling and an increased focus on social prescribing in mental health, now is a good time to discuss the changing landscape of the therapeutic space. Chapter 6 illustrates how the healing space does not have to be confined to an office-based setting. The purpose of this chapter is to examine therapy in alternative environments. We will discuss online counselling, along with ecotherapy; the latter is a form of therapy that acknowledges and appreciates the restorative and healing properties of nature and the natural world.

Research plays an important role in counselling and psychotherapy. The purpose of Chapter 7 is to introduce key issues in this area. This chapter will address the following questions: Does counselling work? And if so, how does it work? Can counselling be harmful to a person? Which types of therapy are best suited to specific problems? This chapter will explain ways of acquiring knowledge – how we know what we know, including a description of the principles of the scientific method. The difference between qualitative and quantitative research approaches will be briefly described. Ten takeaways from talk therapy research will be included in this chapter.

Professional issues will be discussed in Chapter 8. This chapter will examine ways to be safe, effective counsellors, and how to exercise a duty of care to clients. Defining the role of a therapist, explaining boundaries in the therapeutic relationship and ethical issues will be discussed. Throughout this chapter, readers will gain insight into key issues essential to becoming a professional counsellor.

WRITING STYLE AND TERMS OF REFERENCE

My goal in writing this book is to present a summary of the vast amount of academic literature and research about counselling theory and practice that is concise, evidence-based and informative. The writing style is informal, conversational, making it easy to understand and accessible to everyone.

A caveat here – this book provides an overview of the major approaches and discusses some of the key topics in contemporary talk therapy rather than offering a comprehensive guide to counselling.

A word on terminology – professional helpers have different titles and there are several areas of overlap in the theory and practice of counselling and psychotherapy. In the following chapters, counselling and psychotherapy will be referred to interchangeably, as will the terms counsellor and therapist.

ABOUT THE AUTHOR

I feel it's important to say a little about my professional background at this point. From my early adult life, I have been interested in how people cope with problems, such as loss, grief, stress, and emotional pain – the things we all face at some point in our lives. I have spent most of my adult life studying human development and behaviour. Prior to studying psychology, I completed my training as a psychotherapist. Over the years, I have worked with a variety of client groups. After completing my training in person-centred counselling,

I studied cognitive behavioural therapy. Other approaches, such as solution-focused therapy and motivational interviewing, were part of my professional development. My counselling practice adopts a pluralistic approach, selecting the approach most suitable to the client at the time. As a senior lecturer in higher education, I have taught on counselling and psychology courses and designed and delivered postgraduate programmes in the field of psychotherapy.

ACKNOWLEDGEMENTS

I would like to thank the many clients I have worked with throughout the years who have contributed to my development as a therapist. I am also grateful to the many students I have had the pleasure of teaching. I'd also like to thank Lucy Kennedy and the production team at Routledge for making this book possible. A huge thank you to my daughter Claire for providing insightful feedback on early drafts and being a constant source of encouragement, and a big thank you to my husband, James Percival, for his unwavering love and support.

1

COUNSELLING – PAST, PRESENT AND FUTURE

INTRODUCTION

Let's talk about counselling. As a treatment, research shows that both counselling and psychotherapy are effective ways for an individual to increase their ability to cope with psychological distress and emotional pain and to improve their quality of life.[1] There is nothing new there. Still, following a review of several studies on the effectiveness of counselling and psychotherapy, Wampold and Imel (2015)[2] tells us that 80% of those who receive psychotherapy are better off than those who choose not to seek help for their problems. Demand for online counselling increased by 124% in 2020.[3] The good news is that we believe that the stigma that was once associated with seeing a therapist has decreased over the years, which means that more people feel more comfortable asking for help.

We can see a positive move towards wellness recently, focusing on enhancing well-being (even in large corporate environments) and being connected to the environment and each other while flourishing and engaging in meaningful experiences. Every time you turn on the television or radio or open a newspaper or news site, or browse through social media, people are speaking about their mental health and personal struggles and are sharing strategies and tips for wellness.

DOI: 10.4324/9781003196471-1

It's all good news: Promoting good mental health and wellness is always welcome.

However, it is not all good news for some. When people are upset or distressed for some time or have a problem they are struggling with, they usually try to resolve it themselves. Sometimes that works for them. Many times, it does not. While often welcome, tips on wellness and well-meaning suggestions from friends and family do not help. When someone cannot make themselves feel better, they try to get help by discussing the problem with a counsellor or a therapist. Counsellors are professionals trained in various approaches and have different ways of working with people, depending on their experience and worldview of human development. Unless you have been to counselling or spoken to anyone who went to a therapist, you will not know what is involved. This chapter is a good place to start as we explain the historical roots of counselling and some practical details of what is involved in therapy: It will explain what counselling can and cannot do. First, let us look at how counselling and psychotherapy have evolved into today's professional discipline.

COUNSELLING – REFLECTING ON THE PAST

Counselling, as we know it, is a form of emotional support for individuals as well as a method of enhancing personal growth that emerged in western industrial societies and is a healing practice unique to them. It might seem to be a modern phenomenon, but, in fact, the history of 'talk therapy' goes back as far as tribal times when people gathered to share their experiences through stories and the religious practice of confession by priests.[4] Throughout history, perspectives and treatments for mental health have evolved. Ancient cultures believed people with mental illness were possessed by evil spirits, demons, and supernatural forces. The Greek physician Hippocrates, in the fourth century, thought that four essential bodily humors were responsible for mental instability. Historically treatments for mental illness were often violent, painful and dangerous.[5]

The practice of counselling and psychotherapy has only really grown in popularity since the second half of the 20th century. Still, the roots of contemporary counselling go back to the 18th century, a period of social and economic change, which, as McLeod (2013) reminds us, was a turning point in human development, in the way people thought about and lived their lives. Industrialisation saw the 'unchaining' of patients in asylums and more humane treatments offered. Phillippe Pinel (1745–1828), known as the father of modern psychiatry, introduced moral treatment, a psychosocial approach to the care of patients. Pinel encouraged clinicians to adopt a caring, friendly attitude towards patients and to prescribe physical activities and purposeful manual work to help those with mental health issues.[6]

Advances in understanding and theories of mental health and a move away from the psychiatry and medical interventions and treatments appeared in the late 1800s early 1900s with Freud's psychoanalysis (Chapter 2). Freud's approach is widely recognised as the foundation of talk therapy as we know it today.[7] The terms counselling and psychotherapy may give rise to some confusion. Counselling and psychotherapy evolved from academic psychology and are two traditions of theory and practice that are separate yet closely interconnected.[8] The professionals working in this field have different titles and use different terms for similar therapies and roles for people trying to achieve the same thing – helping people with emotional or psychological distress. So, what is the difference? The difference is the theoretical traditions in which they are trained. To fully appreciate the developments in talk therapy over the past 100 years, let us look at the history of psychology, as counselling and psychotherapy are practical applications of psychological theories.

THE PSYCHOLOGY OF COUNSELLING

Wilhelm Wundt established the Institute for Experimental Psychology at the University of Leipzig in Germany in 1879. His was the first laboratory dedicated to psychology and is said to be the beginning of modern psychology. In the early years of psychology, the emergence and development of one approach to understanding human development usually evolved as we rejected another approach.[9]

The development of 'behaviourism,' developed by John Watson, questioned the utility of Wundt's theory of introspection, which focused on subjective, internal thoughts and images of an individual's mental world. Introspection, according to behaviourists, was not amenable to scrutiny and self-reports of thoughts and was unable to be measured objectively. The publication of Watson's *Behaviourist Manifesto* was a turning point in the discipline of psychology. Watson wanted to make psychology a scientific study of human development, adopting scientific principles and methods. Other key figures in behaviourism were Ivan Pavlov and B.F. Skinner (see Chapter 4). Committed to scientific methods and experimentation, Skinner developed the 'laws of learning' and introduced the concept of positive and negative reinforcement. Skinner argued that behaviours could be learned, and his theory went on to have a significant impact on treating challenging and negative behaviours (behaviour modification). The idea of learning is a cornerstone in behavioural therapy and a key component of cognitive behavioural therapy (Chapter 4). Cognitive psychology emerged as a reaction to the dominance of behaviourism. This area of psychology is defined as the scientific study of the thinking mind. Its focus is on helping us understand how we learn, acquire, process and store information. Humanistic psychology, in the 1950s referred to as the 'third force,' opposed behavioural and cognitive theories of human functioning. Humanistic psychologists emphasise the importance of human experience, purpose and meaning.[10]

Demand for therapy

The demand for psychiatric and psychological therapies increased after World War II when returning army veterans reported distressing symptoms of what was then called 'shell shock.' We now refer to this condition as post-traumatic stress disorder (PTSD).[11] Efforts to understand the condition and to alleviate symptoms of neurological, psychological, and physiological responses to trauma resulted in 'systematic desensitisation,' developed by Joseph Wolpe in 1947.[12] Behaviour modification became a popular treatment for fear-induced conditions, such as anxiety and phobias but was criticised as therapy by humanistic psychologists because they believed it ignored the individual's inner world and emotional responses.

Moving through the 20th century, the desire for talking therapy increased. Albert Ellis, influenced mainly by his own negative experiences in childhood, believed that human misery is fuelled by unrealistic expectations. He founded what he called 'Rational Emotive Therapy' based on the theory that how a person thinks about themselves, or events, influences their emotional responses. Some thoughts are irrational, and there was a need to challenge those thoughts to change the emotional response. For Ellis, 'hassles are never really terrible unless you make them so.' Cognitive therapy focuses on the impact of negative and dysfunctional thoughts on people's behavioural and emotional responses to situations or events, a view firmly held by Aaron Beck[13] (Chapter 4). Separate schools of therapy evolved along with the individual approaches in the 1950s and 1960s. Carl Rogers developed person-centred therapy, an approach to helping from a humanistic perspective (Chapter 3). Rogers believed that the aim of therapy was to create a therapeutic environment which would facilitate personal growth and purpose in life.[14]

DIAGNOSIS AND SYMPTOMS

Counselling, as we know it today, came about as some of the great thinkers began to reject the dominance of the medical model in treating emotional distress. In the medical model of mental health, a patient usually has to have a clinical diagnosis of a mental health condition to receive care. Doctors and psychiatrists diagnose a mental health condition or disorder from the *Diagnostic and Statistical Manual of Mental Health Disorders* (DSM-5).[15] The DSM was created to help clinicians communicate with each other. The first edition of the DSM was published in 1952. Before this, the data on mental health was collected and recorded under the title, *The Statistical*

Manual for the Use of Institutions for the Insane. The original publication of the DSM had 22 diagnoses.[16] The DSM categorises mental health based on a checklist of symptoms, with a graded dimension – mild, moderate or severe. The manual is reviewed periodically. The problem is that there are gaps in our understanding of mental health, and there are heated debates and controversies around categorising mental health conditions. If thresholds for diagnoses continue to be lowered, more categories will be added to the DSM, resulting in an overmedicalisation of mental health. Consider this: What is the difference between depression and sadness and anxiety and fear? Is it the length of time you have experienced symptoms, the intensity of the symptoms or the impact symptoms have on your daily life and relationships? Could talking to someone, a trained expert, help?

COUNSELLING – WHAT IS IT, AND WHAT IS INVOLVED?

You are reading this book because you want to learn more about counselling. You may be thinking of looking for help for a problem or an issue in your life. Or perhaps you are contemplating studying and training as a therapist yourself. Either way, you will have your own idea of what counselling is all about. You might have been influenced by friends or family who has spoken about their own experiences in counselling, or you may have formed your ideas about counselling and therapy from the media. Here, a word of caution – media portrayals generally show a therapist and client interacting dramatically, which can fuel misperceptions of what happens in therapy. The media portrayal of therapy can, unfortunately, influence viewers, consciously or unconsciously, on whether or not to seek help when needed. My aim in writing this book is to clarify any misconceptions or misunderstandings about counselling and explain what counselling involves. Let us start with a formal definition of counselling from the British Association of Counselling and Psychotherapy (BACP)[17]

Therapy provides a safe and confidential space for you to talk to a trained professional about your issues and concerns. Your therapist will help you explore your thoughts, feelings, and behaviours to better understand yourself and others.

This definition clarifies that counselling is fundamentally about one person talking about their problems and another person listening. While that may sound pretty simple, the practice is anything but straightforward. Counselling and psychotherapy are characterised by the presence of a 'competent other.' This trained professional has the aptitude and the skills necessary to facilitate a meaningful conversation about the issue(s) at hand. It is crucial for a therapist to listen effectively in a deliberate and structured way. Even though listening is not always easy, it can be one of the most powerful skills we acquire during counsellor training. If you learn how to listen effectively, you will be able to build stronger relationships and enhance your ability to help others. Communication, interpersonal and social skills are essential in counselling and other roles that use counselling skills, but not as the primary function. For example, teachers, social workers, nurses, doctors and even police officers all use counselling skills. However, being a skilled listener is only one aspect of counselling. Positive personality traits such as compassion, kindness and patience are the other foundations of counselling skills. A great deal of evidence suggests that personal characteristics play a crucial role in effective counselling[18].

WHY DO PEOPLE LOOK FOR HELP FROM A COUNSELLOR?

There are many reasons why one might want to see a therapist. Some people are dealing with personal dilemmas or difficulties in interpersonal relationships. Others are experiencing distress or disturbance with a transition or loss in their lives or struggling with low self-esteem or trauma in their childhood. Someone might be feeling lost in their life and wants to talk about their decision-making process in a safe and confidential setting. Sometimes, people need help coping with chronic illnesses or debilitating pain conditions. Clients might feel angry, ashamed, guilty, sad or lonely, which negatively affects their daily lives, leading to feelings of being stuck. Regardless of the reason for coming to therapy, counselling can help people with complex and challenging situations by exploring their feelings and experiences in a calm, non-judgemental space and helping bring about positive change.

CHILDHOOD EXPERIENCES AND WELL-BEING IN ADULTHOOD

As I mentioned, there are many reasons why people want to talk to a therapist. At the very start, the therapist needs to get a sense of who a client is. The first session focuses on gathering information about the issue that is troubling the client and recording their biographical information and, often, their relevant medical history. It is not unusual for clients to share details about their family and their childhood experiences as they try to understand the reasons for their current emotional state. The why is essential for some people: They question why they feel the way they do or behave in ways that cause problems and tension for themselves and others. As human beings, we like to make close links between our past and our current lives, and we try to understand ourselves and make sense of our experiences. The question is, how important is the past in our current problems? How much do childhood experiences, negative and positive, impact our health and well-being in later life? Of course, our relationships with our parents or caregivers in our early years are important for our physical, emotional and social development. Lots of research has supported this idea.[19]

In a landmark study by Kaiser Permanente and the Centres for Disease Control and Prevention in the United States, 'The Adverse Childhood Experiences Study' (between 1995 and 1997), 17,337 people (54% female, 46% male) answered questions about physical, emotional and sexual abuse, absence or separation from parents, living in a home with a parent who had a mental illness and domestic violence in their childhood (before the age of 18 years). The results found that exposure to adverse events during childhood increased the likelihood of experiencing negative mental and physical health in adulthood, such as depression, substance abuse, diabetes and severe obesity.[20]

Further research found that childhood neglect and trauma are related to social and cognitive functioning delays and poor educational attainment. Fellini and colleagues expanded the categories of adverse childhood experiences (ACEs), including community violence, racism and child poverty. The researchers argue that a child's developing brain does not distinguish between threats inside or outside the home or immediate family. In other words, children respond to threats both in their internal and external environments.

Positive childhood experiences

Several studies have highlighted an important point, that is, that the past neither defines us nor binds us; our childhood experiences do not have to determine who we are or what we will become. We cannot change our childhood experiences, but we can change our responses to those experiences. Otherwise, counselling and psychotherapy would be ultimately futile, and we know that's not true. It is also important to note that children's well-being and development result from complex interactions of biological and environmental influences, both positive and negative, which influence later life. To fully understand the impact of childhood experiences on our adult lives, it is important to consider the effects of positive childhood experiences.

Research shows that positive childhood experiences (PCEs) shape brain development and the internal stress response system.[21] Successful attachment during the first years of life is important, as first claimed by John Bowlby's 'Attachment Theory.' The presence of a safe, stable, nurturing relationship and environment during childhood is vital for optimal development in adulthood. Research tells us that positive parenting – high levels of parent–child connections, parental warmth and responsiveness is linked to greater emotional well-being and lower risk of mental health and physical health outcomes in later life. Positive experiences in childhood, including having supportive relationships with family and friends, a sense of belonging to a social group and feeling safe and protected, are critical.

In 2019, a team of researchers, led by Christina Bethell, found a link between positive childhood events and mental health and relationships amongst adults who had also experienced adverse childhood events.[22] The researchers define positive childhood experiences as feeling safe and protected in the family environment, feeling cared for by at least two non-parent adults, participating in activities and being able to express feelings openly. The findings suggest social and emotional support during childhood are protective factors against poor mental health in adulthood.

In 2019, Yamaoka and Bard found that the number of ACEs was associated with social-emotional deficits and developmental delay risks in early childhood.[23] Despite this finding, positive parenting practices exhibited robust protection independent of adverse childhood experiences. Recent research has found that strong childhood relationships in families were associated with greater flourishing in adulthood regardless of negative childhood experiences. While the research on positive childhood events is promising, we need more research to further our understanding. However, the research already shows that positive childhood experiences can buffer against adverse events and promote healthy development. Additionally, early childhood is the period when harm can be prevented or mitigated even when there is a risk from adverse experiences. It appears from emerging research that the concept of reliance is important in mitigating the impact of adverse childhood experiences. You can read more about this on the website of the aptly named HOPE Research Center (Healthy Outcomes from Positive Experiences) at the University of Oklahoma.

Research has shown that toxic stress can alter and damage a child's brain structure and function.[24] Thankfully, the human brain can change and adapt to new experiences, a concept known as neuroplasticity.[25]

This is excellent news, and it reinforces something we knew already: Human beings are resilient. Researchers interested in resilience have found that a positive attitude, establishing trusting relationships and asking for help can all contribute to resilience and paying attention to emotions can help people cope better with negative emotions and improve their lives.

HOW CAN COUNSELLING HELP?

We know that seeking social and emotional support when confronted with difficulties and challenges is a worthwhile endeavour for some people. Most people expect their counsellors to have all the answers. In reality, they do not have the answer to all of your problems, nor will they tell you what to do. Instead, the therapist will listen to you and respond to whatever issues you bring to the session. Remember, counsellors and therapists do not provide a diagnosis of a mental health condition. Even though some therapies involve more active collaboration between the therapist and the client, for example, in cognitive behaviour therapy, which we will look at in greater detail in Chapter 4, a therapist will not impose their views or voice their opinion on a client's behaviour or thought process. Generally speaking, individuals go to therapy to gain insight into their thoughts and behavioural patterns and reflect on their relationships and life choices. The changes that can be brought about by counselling include a shift in perspective, new insight, new ways of thinking and behaving in situations and in relationships, self-awareness, an enhanced capacity to tolerate and regulate emotional responses and learning new ways to respond and not react to adverse events or challenging interpersonal relationships.

DAY ONE IN THERAPY

What happens on day one? Every counsellor begins their first meeting with a client in their own way. Typically, the first appointment is a consultation where the counsellor introduces themselves and explains how they work. The client might ask questions about the qualifications and experience of the counsellor and clarify any issues they have regarding the counselling process. Counsellors usually like to discuss ways in which they may be able to help. If the therapist and the client agree to go forward together, issues around scheduling appointments, cancellations and costs are discussed and agreed upon. This is often referred to as a contract which can be verbal or written. The therapist will explain how they will respect your privacy, the confidentiality of the information you disclose and how they will securely store notes from each session. The counsellor will also explain the limits to confidentiality if they feel there is a risk to the client's safety or others. As part of the first session, it is important to discuss when to evaluate the process and progress of therapy. When this 'housekeeping' part of the consultation is over, the therapist will ask you about your reasons for coming to therapy.

How long does that first appointment last? That varies with the counsellor and the therapeutic approach they like to take, but it usually takes approximately an hour. The frequency of therapy varies, too, according to the needs of a client and the type of therapy on offer. You and your therapist will agree on how often you should come back. You might see your counsellor on your own or as a couple, or as a family and counselling can take place face-to-face in the therapist's office or clinic or online via video or telephone.[26]

THE ROLE OF THE COUNSELLOR

What does a counsellor do? A counsellor's role varies depending on their therapeutic approach, the strategy you have agreed upon and the nature of the issue. Some qualities are common to all counsellors, including the ability to listen, be patient and have an empathic understanding of another person's life, be compassionate to another person's struggles and suffering, be kind, respectful and have a genuine interest in how people cope and live with emotional pain and distress.

Therapists work within their level of competence and training, and whatever framework or approach is appropriate for the client and their specific issues, considering their particular needs, goals and perceptions. Chapters 2–4 will examine different approaches to therapy and describe the various methods counsellors use to help their clients.

Every counsellor knows that their role is a privileged one. In my own experience as a therapist for over 20 years, the work has been enormously rewarding and, at times, challenging. There are occasions when you know that you have connected in a meaningful way with a client. Dave Mearns and Mick Cooper, both leading and influential figures in counselling, call this 'relational depth.' This is defined as 'moments of in-depth encounter' or 'profound contact and engagement with another.'[27] While this sense of deep engagement with another person can occur in everyday life, Cooper refers to this experience taking place in therapy. Relational depth is an intuitive sense that the therapist and the client have when they connect in the therapeutic space.

COUNSELLING – THE FUTURE DIRECTIONS

Advances in technology drive our society, so it is not surprising that our counselling and psychotherapy services are part of a global initiative to improve and increase access to those services for those who need them. The COVID-19 pandemic has accelerated the transition to online video and telephone counselling. Some people, who were used to seeing their therapist face-to-face, found moving to the small screen of their phone or computer to be a significant change and challenging, but many seem to have adapted well overall. Internet searches for online counselling rose by 124% during 2020 compared to the previous year.[28] This might result from global uncertainty, but the public perception and willingness to use online counselling also show an increased need for counselling services and a shift in attitude about a therapeutic space.

Further advances in technology in counselling and psychotherapy will provide clients and therapists opportunities and challenges.

Training in counselling and psychotherapy, whether university-led or by private providers, will need to evolve. Those who develop and design curricula may need to consider changing and adopting modules in cyber counselling and rethink their protocols for placements on professional courses.

COUNSELLING, PSYCHOTHERAPY AND ARTIFICIAL INTELLIGENCE

The interaction between psychology and technology using artificial intelligence (AI) is constantly developing and evolving. This is a significant growth area in the corporate world and the use of AI chatbots. It is not only about a changing landscape or a changing therapeutic space; it is a change in the therapist delivering care and support.[29] Your therapist, a robot called Wysa or Eliza, will work in partnership with you independent of a human therapist. Computer-mediated psychotherapy offers so much more than just connecting patients to therapists via live video chat: Virtual therapy has begun to emerge as a means to support a range of emotional and psychological processes.

By embracing both a text-based and screen-based interface, the new technology represents an exciting fusion of a therapeutic environment with easy access, unattended by a professional and always available. Yes, AI has potential opportunities for psychotherapy through applications such as chatbots and apps that help record mood and anxiety ratings. Nevertheless, the use of AI programmes raises important ethical and clinical concerns that have yet to be adequately addressed. In addition to clients seeking help, therapists are also challenged by this since most of us value the relationship with our clients and its effect on their positive change. It is not something we would easily hand over to a robot. Talk therapy has come a long way since priests' confessionals, and the smoke-filled rooms in Vienna where Freud pondered the inner conflicts and tensions buried deep within us. It is important to remember that regardless of divisions, separate schools of thought and diverse philosophical assumptions about human suffering and misery, therapy is essentially about the human condition, the lived experience.

CONCLUSIONS

Counselling and psychotherapy include a range of non-medical therapies designed to help people with psychological, social, and emotional problems. Professional therapists may have different titles, depending on their training and philosophical position in understanding human development. I hope you have gained an understanding that a therapist does not advise or tell a client what to do. The therapeutic space is for reflection, exploration, emotional and psychological growth and facilitating change. The lifelong negative implications resulting from adverse childhood events are well established. From recent research, we have also learned that positive relationships with significant others in childhood are crucial to optimising our well-being and health in later life. Positive experiences during the early years can serve as a protective factor against poor mental health in later life. Adverse childhood events do not bind us; instead, positive experiences in childhood can buffer us against the harmful impact of negative experiences. Research from neuroscience has shown that brain plasticity permits anatomical brain structures to change and adapt to new learning and new experiences. The concept of *change* is a crucial issue in counselling: We can confidently say that the past does not *have* to hold us captive.

NOTES

1 Cooper (2008)
2 Wampold and Imel (2015)
3 Hazlegreaves (2020)
4 McLeod (2013)
5 McLeod (2013)
6 Weiner (1992)
7 McLeod (2013)
8 McLeod (2013)

9 Schultz and Schultz (2015)
10 Schultz and Schultz (2015)
11 Fischer (2012)
12 Schultz and Schultz (2015)
13 Kennerley et al. (2017)
14 Claringbull (2010)
15 American Psychiatric Association (2013)
16 Crocq and Crocq (2000)
17 British Association of Counselling and Psychotherapy (BACP 2013)
18 Clements-Hickman and Reese (2022)
19 Felitti et al. (1998)
20 Felitti et al. (1998)
21 Rayce et al. (2017)
22 Bethell et al. (2019)
23 Yamaoka and Bard (2019)
24 Teicher (2006)
25 Lillard and Erisir (2011)
26 Kennedy and Charles (2002)
27 Mearns and Cooper (2017)
28 Hazlegreaves (2020)
29 Xu and Zhuang (2020)

2

FREUD PSYCHOANALYSIS REVIEWED AND RECONSIDERED

Over the years, talk therapy and psychoanalysis have been synonymous with the iconic image of a therapist analysing a person reclining on a couch. This book's cover features a couch as a tribute to Sigmund Freud, the creator of psychoanalysis – a therapeutic method that dates back to the 1800s – and the founder of talk therapy. As we go through the chapter, we will examine the reasoning behind Freud's selection of a couch for therapy. Freud is a renowned and contentious figure in the field of contemporary psychology. His substantial contributions to the creation of psychoanalytic theory and its application to human behaviour and psychological health are at the core of our present-day knowledge. His concepts about the human psyche, such as the unconscious mind, continue to be highly influential in some therapeutic approaches. Even though many people know the words 'denial,' 'repression' and 'slips of the tongue,' they might not realise that these terms are linked to Freud's idea of unconscious mind, a concept that is fundamental to psychoanalytic theory and practice. We will begin this chapter by taking a look at Freud's ideas about human nature. Then, we will review psychoanalysis in practice.

DOI: 10.4324/9781003196471-2

BACKGROUND

Sigmund Freud was born on May 6th, 1856, in Moravia, which is now a part of the Czech Republic; he was the oldest of eight children from a Jewish family. In 1860, Freud's family moved to Vienna, where he lived most of his life before relocating to London in later life. After his graduation from medical school, he specialised in mental health. In the beginning of his career, he focused on neurological problems and the nervous system. During his internship in Paris with neurologist Jean Martin Charcot, he developed an interest in adopting hypnosis as a treatment for hysteria and neurosis. After developing his own theories and methods for addressing nervous disorders, he established his own practice in 1886. After his father's death in 1897, Freud began self-analysis, which included dedicating some part of every day to this process. The purpose of this process was both personal and professional. A large portion of this self-reflection involved interpreting his dreams which eventually led to the creation of his most renowned work – the publication of The Interpretation of Dreams. Despite its initial criticism, this book marked a new era in the psychoanalytic movement, and Freud earned international recognition. Freud was a prolific writer. Even after being diagnosed with cancer in 1923, he continued reviewing and revising his theories until his death in London in 1939.[1] Numerous biographies have been written about Freud. Peter Gay (1998) provides a comprehensive look at the social and political environment in which he lived, as well as his progressive views on human personality.

FREUD'S VIEW OF HUMAN NATURE

According to Freud, the first five years of a person's life are crucial to their behaviour and psychological wellness as adults. He claimed that from birth to six years, human beings are affected by uncontrollable elements, repressed intentions, as well as biological and instinctive desires (psychosexual development which we will look at later in this chapter). Innate biological instincts and drives are a major part of his theory. Initially, he described sexual energy as 'libido' but later extended the term to incorporate all life instincts. This was necessary to ensure the survival of individuals and humankind. In addition, instincts stimulate us to advance, develop and be innovative. As such, libido encompasses more than just sexual energy. Freud believed that human beings were driven to seek pleasure and avoid pain, just like other living beings. Furthermore, Freud also discussed death instincts, which he referred to as the concealed longing to expire or to harm others. According to Freud, both aggression and sexual drive are key in understanding our behaviour.[2]

A STRUCTURAL MODEL OF THE MIND

According to Sigmund Freud, the unconscious mind is a powerful force in the shaping of our personalities. He believed that this part of the mind stores feelings, memories and desires that are not accessible to us in the present. He further stated that our unconscious mind is where we conceal our deepest fears, desires and impulses. Freud described the conscious mind as being similar to the tip of an iceberg, representing only a small proportion of what is inside the mind. The conscious mind consists of our current awareness, while the preconscious part encompasses our stored memories, fantasies and emotions, although they may not be immediately available. Freud compared the unconscious aspect of the mind to the largest part of the iceberg, which lies beneath the surface and is invisible. Freud went further to divide the mind into three distinct yet related concepts – the id, the ego and the superego – each with a separate function as illustrated next.[3]

THE ID

The id is the motivating force behind our desires, giving us instinctive reactions to life and its happenings and we don't think about the possible outcomes. It is said that the id is the source of pleasure-seeking and self-gratification of people, which encourages them to fulfil their wants and needs. The pleasure principle directs the id, which is that element by which individuals are driven by their desire to acquire enjoyment and avoid suffering. This can lead to counterproductive behaviour, as people may act in ways that are not in their best interests, merely because they offer instant gratification. People may take part in dangerous activities without considering the repercussions. Freud's theory states that the id is balanced by the ego and the superego.[4]

THE EGO

The ego develops from the id and functions as an intermediary between the id and the superego. Guided by the reality principle, it is the most malleable and adjustable of the three components. It is the segment of the personality that is most inclined to be conscious of other individuals' ideas and emotions, and it is also most likely to be able to see things from someone else's point of view.[5]

THE SUPEREGO

The superego is the ethical component of the personality, which helps people in controlling their impulses and selecting options that agree with their beliefs. The superego is the result of the ego taking in the values and standards of their environment. This aspect of the personality can be seen as a moral compass, directing the ego in its decision-making. The superego is formed in response to the demands of society and is shaped by an individual's encounters and interactions with others. Socialisation is the process through which the superego is developed. As children, we become acquainted with the expectations and regulations of our environment, we internalise these values and standards. The superego is ever evolving as people confront new experiences and knowledge. The superego serves a few functions. It gives people a sense of right and wrong and propels them to act in accordance with social expectations, and it operates as a regulator, curbing the id's desires.[6]

PSYCHOSEXUAL DEVELOPMENT

Freud's theory of psychosexual development was controversial and continues to divide opinions within counselling and psychotherapy to this day. His theory of psychosexual theory outlined five stages of development from infancy to adulthood. These are the oral, anal, phallic, latent and genital stages. During these stages, individuals encounter struggles and pressures that are associated with erogenous zones and that are subject to under gratification or over gratification of needs at one of the stages, which could result in a person becoming fixated at that stage. Additionally, he maintained that how someone deals with these conflicts during every stage of growth may have a lasting effect on their character and behaviour in adulthood in an unconscious manner.

The stages of Freud's psychosexual development theory are as follows.

(1) *Oral stage*: During the oral stage, which spans from birth to one year, babies take pleasure in sucking and chewing on objects.
(2) *Anal stage*: From one to three years, the anal stage is marked by the sensation they experience in relation to toilet training.
(3) *Phallic stage*: During the phallic stage, lasting from three to six years, children become aware that they derive pleasure from their genitals and may also develop the Oedipus complex where young boys feel attracted to their mothers and feel competitive towards their fathers.
(4) *Latency stage*: Once the latency period begins, from six years to the age of puberty, sexual impulses are subdued as the child invests in building relationships with others.
(5) *Genital stage*: Finally, when puberty hits, the genital stage is initiated, and individuals are capable of engaging in sexual relationships with others.

Though each phase of psychosexual development has been highly influential in the field of psychology, the theory has also been criticised for its emphasis on sexual urges and its lack of consideration for other factors that influence personality development, such as social and cultural factors.[7]

PSYCHOANALYSIS IN PRACTICE

There has been much debate on the appropriateness of therapists disclosing their own personal information to their clients and the effects this may have on therapy outcomes. In some instances, it may be suitable for therapists to share personal information or experience if it could help the client in understanding a concept or come to terms with a challenging emotional reaction. In classical psychoanalysis, self-disclosure is not encouraged. The analyst maintains a detached attitude during the therapy session, refraining from disclosing too much personal information which leads to the successful implementation of strategies like free association, transference and analysing the dreams of the client.

FREE ASSOCIATION

Clients usually go for therapy to understand the cause of their difficulties and to develop the ability to cope with future problems. With this in mind, it is imperative that the therapist provides a secure and safe space for the client to express their painful and often disturbing thoughts, memories and impulses without fear. As mentioned earlier, the image of a couch is synonymous with Freud. He advocated that the client be relaxed, lying on a couch out of direct line of sight of the therapist so that the client could not gauge the therapist's response to anything they said. This context supported the procedure of free association, which he argued was a fundamental rule of psychoanalysis. When engaging in free association, individuals are urged to express anything that comes into their mind, no matter how insignificant or uncomfortable it may be. Freud believed that when a client is free to express thoughts and words or recall events, important information can eventually emerge, which can enable the therapist to infer and explore further meanings and connections from their past experiences to their present difficulties. The process of free association also allows past experiences to become more vivid and enables blocked feelings to be released.[8] Free association was not Freud's only psychoanalytic technique. Freud used transference as well as dream interpretation to help clients unlock unconscious motivations and reasons for their distress.

TRANSFERENCE

Based on his own observations in his clinical practice, Freud claimed that the therapeutic relationship was significant in helping people to understand the origin of their distress. He believed that the way in which the client perceived the analyst mirrored emotional and relational issues in both their past and present lives. Freud noticed that his client's perceptions of him did not match his actual behaviour or attitude. The client built strong views of him that were not grounded in reality. Freud realised that his clients were interpreting him through a filter developed from their prior relationships, with emotions being transferred or projected onto him from those associations. This transference was determined by the patient's relationship with significant people in life – for example a strict father or an overprotective mother.[9]

DREAM ANALYSIS

Freud firmly established the concept of dream analysis, often interpreting his own dreams to illustrate this. The most notable elements of his dream theory were the ideas of wish fulfilment and drive discharge, the necessity of avoiding the dream censor and the differentiation between manifest (what it appears to be) and latent (repressed thoughts) content. Freud believed that dreams symbolise a concealed satisfaction of the fulfilment of a repressed wish and that they are the clearest path to the unconscious; in fact, he said that dreams were the royal road to the unconscious. According to him, dreams originated from personal experiences, but were not exactly life-like, instead embodying hidden wants and desires. As dreams usually reflect suppressed longings and are an insight into the unconscious, the role of the psychoanalyst is to interpret a client's dreams to help them understand their concealed wishes.[10]

DIVISION AND DERISION

Freud's ideas about psychoanalysis were highly contentious, causing both internal and external debates. He expected and demanded that his colleagues who practiced psychoanalysis accept and fully support his ideas and concepts. Any deviations from his beliefs were met with disapproval. Claringbull reminds us that this division and split with the psychoanalytic community in the early years are often referred to as the Freud Wars due to the intense animosity created.[11] Breuer was the first to vocalise his doubts about infantile sexuality, deeming it to be baseless and extreme. Carl Jung, who was once regarded as Freud's protégé, contested the idea that personality is set in childhood and instead argued that spiritual and non-material aspects should also be considered. Others distanced themselves from Freud and proposed their own theories. Notable figures like Erik Erikson established eight phases of psychosocial development theory which introduced social and cultural aspects into his lifespan development theory. Melanie Klein formed object relations theory.[12]

Outside of the psychoanalytic community, British psychologist Hans Eysenck was Freud's strongest critic, claiming that psychoanalysis was no more than subjective speculation and dismissing his theories as unscientific and unfalsifiable. In his 1954 article, 'The Nature of Psychoanalysis,' Eysenck claimed that Freud's theories of the unconscious are vague and lacked any empirically based evidence. He further suggests that the psychoanalytic approach is too focused on the past and fails to consider the future, which he believed to be an essential part of psychological treatment. Eysenck's article was groundbreaking in its criticism of Freud and has had a lasting impact on the field. An extensive critique of Freud's theories can be found in Eysenck's book, *Decline and Fall of the Freudian Empire* (2004).

ANNA FREUD

Although many disagreed with Freud's theories, leading to a split in the psychoanalytic community, Freud's daughter Anna (1895–1982) remained loyal to her father and sought to further the field of psychoanalysis. Anna Freud became known as a Neo-Freudian and is best remembered for her work with children and the establishment of play therapy. While others like Hermine von hug-Hellmuth, Carl Jung, Lou Andreas-Salome and Sandor Ferenczi had already initiated child therapy, Anna was the first to develop and standardise it. She argued that that therapy should not be conducted on children until they reach the latency phase of psychosexual development. She esteemed and valued the children she worked with and also regarded them as unique persons and worked hard to establish a trusting therapeutic rapport with her young clients. She believed that children's drawings were an external expression of their emotions.[13]

In addition to her work with children, Anna believed that the ego had more potential than what was initially proposed by her father, and she created ego psychology. One of the ego's tasks is to reduce anxiety, and it has several strategies – known as defense mechanisms – at its disposal to do this. In order to understand some defence mechanisms, let's summarise what Freud said about anxiety.

Freud claimed that our anxiety is triggered from the moment we are separated from our mother at birth, which he referred to as the birth trauma. He argued that this fear is generated from the transition from the security of the mother's womb to the unpredictable nature of the outside world and uncertainty in having our needs satisfied. Freud argued that our subsequent anxieties are all derived from this experience of anxiety. He identified three categories of anxiety, the first being reality anxiety, which is caused by real threats in the environment and can be easily reduced by removing oneself from the source of the danger – for example leaving a burning building or getting out of the way of a moving vehicle.

Neurotic anxiety is the fear that the instincts of the id will over-power the ego, leading to behaviours which could be punished, such as being overly aggressive or succumbing to sexual desires. Moral anxiety on the other hand is the feeling of guilt when someone does something against the values of the super ego. To put it succinctly, anxiety controls our behaviour by causing us to avoid threatening experiences in the environment, to reduce the urgings of the id and to act in accordance with our internalised values. Let us now look at how ego defense mechanisms can protect us from anxiety.

Ego defense mechanisms share two traits: they are unconscious – meaning that they are done without awareness, and they distort and falsify reality. Repression is the most essential of these defense mecha-nisms since it is the first one that the ego will resort to. Repression refers to pushing away uncomfortable or unacceptable thoughts from the conscious mind into the unconscious. Other common defence mechanisms are denial, regression and projection. Denial happens when someone chooses to ignore reality and denies that a problem exists. Regression is reverting to a behaviour which is associated with earlier developmental stages, for instance, displaying child-like behav-iour. Projection involves attributing your own negative feelings to another person – for example believing they don't like you when, in fact, it's the other way around, you don't like them.[14]

PSYCHOANALYSIS AND SCIENCE

We learned earlier that Freud began his career as a neurologist. He had ambitions to become a famous scientist. In his time, the idea that mental issues were due to biological factors was widespread. As a neurologist, Freud attempted to associate neural systems with psychodynamic principles, but this venture was unsuccessful, as ref-erenced in his 'Project for a Scientific Psychology,' which was writ-ten in 1895. He reflected on his project and had varying opinions about his endeavour, considering his work in this area, from being excellent to being a failure. He maintained that neurology could shed light on mental disorders, to the point of calling it 'Psychology for Neurologists' in his conversations with Wilhelm Fliess, Freud's close companion and a controversial figure.[15]

In recent years, others have chosen to revisit Freuds work in light of developments in neuroscience. Mark Solms is renowned for his discovery of the forebrain mechanisms related to dreaming, as well as for his role in bridging psychoanalytic theories and methods with neuroscience. His exploration of Freud's concept of alterations in our consciousness and of unconscious mind emotion and dreaming has provided new perspectives. As both an analyst and a neuropsychologist, he has worked to re-evaluate some of Freud's key principles in relation to modern neuroscience. He has looked into emotional drives, repression and the location of the unconscious in the brain, and how these understandings may be applied to clinical practice. It is said that Solms was the first to utilise the term 'neuropsychoanalysis.' His research is consistent with Freud's beliefs about our innate biological needs and instinctive requirements. Solms' mission is to bring attention to Freud's concept of the unconscious and neural processes in the brain.[16] To date, Solms' research has identified associations between neural pathways with Freud's concept of the id (upper brainstem and limbic systems) and the ego (in the cortex). It should be kept in mind that disagreements and conflicting views did not happen in the early stages of psychoanalytic theories alone. There are conflicting views about the emergence of neuropsychoanalysis, with some considering it to be anti-psychoanalytic.[17]

CONCLUSION

Sigmund Freud is widely recognised in the field of modern psychology. His development of psychoanalytic theory and practice serves as the foundation for our current understanding of human behaviour and mental health. His ideas about the human psyche, including the unconscious mind, still have a strong influence. Freud's pioneering work in psychoanalysis introduced the idea of talk therapy as a way to deal with psychological distress and mental health challenges. Freud believed that early childhood experiences were fundamental in psychological and emotional well-being in adulthood. He argued that repressed memories and emotions in the unconscious mind were a root cause of mental and emotional issues. His psychosexual development theory is a prominent and influential concept of personality development. It argues that during childhood, a person's psyche experiences a series of phases where they focus on different body parts for sexual gratification. This drive for satisfaction is caused by an instinctive force known as libido. Freud's theory and approach to psychoanalysis, as well as his views on child sexuality, are still debated and discussed in the field of psychology. His theories of human nature and the methods of therapy he used have had a significant impact on counselling, psychotherapy, the arts, literature and popular culture. Freud set the stage for the creation of further theories of counselling, in part due to the criticism of his own psychoanalysis. His take on psychotherapy was often seen as pessimistic, and while some of Freud's colleagues modified his original concepts, others had a separate viewpoint on the nature of humanity and the practice of psychotherapy. One school of thought is the humanistic perspective, which views individuals in a positive and optimistic manner. We will now turn our attention to the humanistic approach to human nature and to Carl Rogers, the founder of person-centred therapy.

NOTES

1 Gay (1998)
2 Schultz and Schultz (2015)
3 Barker et al. (2010)
4 Hergenhahn (1994)
5 Monte and Sollod (2003)
6 Hergenhahn (1994)
7 Hergenhahn (1994)
8 Hergenhahn (1994)
9 Claringbull (2010)
10 Monte and Sollod (2003)

11 Claringbull (2010)
12 Monte and Sollod (2003)
13 Monte and Sollod (2003)
14 Schultz and Schultz (2015)
15 Gay (1998)
16 Solms and Turnbull (2011)
17 Yovell et al. (2015)

3

HUMANISTIC PSYCHOLOGY –
A PERSON-CENTRED APPROACH
TO COUNSELLING

INTRODUCTION

In Chapter 2 we saw that Freud, one of the most influential thinkers in the development of counselling and psychotherapy had his own way of working with people in therapy. His approach was based on his own theories which came from his personal views on human development. We learned that he believed that the early years and the basic instinctive drives in children and their relationships with their parents were the most influential factor in mental ill-health in adulthood. Freud and others who you will be introduced to in this book, for example, Ellis and Beck, were influenced by their own unique experiences, their history and the social, cultural and political context of their time.

We are now going to take a look at person-centred therapy, which is a very different approach to psychoanalysis. The prevailing wisdom at that time focused on causes and cures for psychological disorders. Carl Rogers wanted to understand human development from a completely fresh perspective – a humanistic perspective.

HUMANISTIC PSYCHOLOGY

Psychoanalysis and behaviourism were the main schools of therapy in the 1950s and 1960s before humanistic psychology emerged in

DOI: 10.4324/9781003196471-3

America as the 'third force.' Humanistic psychologists told us that from the moment of birth, we have basic physiological needs for food, warmth and shelter and we have the need to be loved and cared for. To be human. We are not only determined to survive, but we are also creative, autonomous beings striving to reach our potential. While Freud focused on the repressed, negative half of human development, inner conflict and unconscious repression, humanistic practitioners focus on the healthy development of an individual.[1] Humanistic thinkers were interested in the individual's own subjective experience; their focus of inquiry was on what we need to thrive and what we can do to be our best selves. Abraham Maslow and Carl Rogers are two names synonymous with humanistic psychology. Maslow, who is considered the founding father of humanistic psychology, wrote, 'what a man can be, he must be; he must be true to his own nature . . . to become everything that one is capable of becoming.'[2] To understand humanistic ideas about personality, we must understand the self-concept. Humanistic psychologists believe that as we reflect upon our life's experiences through the years, we develop more and more individualised selves. Therefore, the self is constantly evolving, and the ultimate purpose of human beings is to realise our potential. Therapists offer various explanations for how this might happen.

This is a positive perspective of human development, and it has influenced lots of approaches in counselling, including person-centred and Gestalt counselling. Although both of these approaches share the same philosophy of human development, they have different ways of working with clients. Let's talk about the person-centred approach founded by Carl Rogers, as he is considered to be the most influential humanistic theorist.[3]

CARL ROGERS

Carl Rogers was born in Chicago in 1902. He was brought up in a strict household and his development as a person was very much influenced by the conservative religious beliefs of his parents. Rogers spent a lot of time on his own as a teenager – his parents discouraged him from making friends or participating in recreational activities outside the family. Educated at Columbia University, Rogers studied psychology for most of his career and became involved with the encounter group movement. At one stage he wanted to enter the ministry and, while he changed his mind about that, he remained dedicated to the fundamental moral principles of his religious background. He believed that people should be respected, unconditional love should be offered to all and forgiveness should be freely given to those who had transgressed.[4]

ROGERS'S VIEW OF HUMAN NATURE

Rogers held an optimistic view of human nature, valuing the uniqueness of each individual. Additionally, he embraced the principle of self-redemption and believed that we are all constantly striving for self-fulfilment. His approach to therapy focused on exploring, enhancing and rediscovering these qualities that are inherent in us all. Rogers was emphatic that human beings are essentially good, even when goodness is not always obvious in our behaviours or thoughts.

The primary focus of Rogers's life's work, and indeed his principal interests, were developing his innovative theories about psychotherapy. As a pioneering counselling theorist and practitioner, Rogers's views on personality evolved from his work with his clients. There were certain fundamental beliefs that shaped his model of personality. He believed that human behaviour was rational, that human nature was essentially positive and that human beings are trustworthy. Rogers's entire body of work is shaped by these beliefs.[5]

PERSON-CENTRED APPROACH IN THEORY

To understand Rogers's person-centred approach to therapy, let's review his theory of human development and personality. The theoretical background to the person-centred approach was published by

Rogers in 1959, and here he introduced the concepts of the actualising tendency and self-concept.

THE ACTUALISING TENDENCY

Although there are some technical terms in Rogers's theory, he explains them well in his writings. To begin with, we need to understand what he called the actualising tendency. This is the basic tenet of his theory and a fundamental element in his approach to therapy. He believed the actualising tendency is a motivational force that exists in all living human beings and he describes it like this:

> There is one central source of energy in the human organism: that is a function of the whole organism rather than some portion of it: and it is perhaps best conceptualised as a tendency toward fulfilment, actualisation, and maintenance and enhancement of the organism.[6]

This tendency towards growth, as Rogers believed, could be thwarted or suppressed, but never destroyed. Rogers believed that human beings have an innate capacity for goodness. We are constantly striving towards fulfilment and motivated to become fully functioning, even when confronted with adversity and when engaging in negative behaviour. The actualising tendency is the driving force behind human development and personality. We may know from our own experiences in the world that this makes intuitive sense. When life is not good, and situations or events are overwhelming, we move forward. We keep going. We may know people personally, or we may know of people who have had horrific experiences in childhood and as adults. They have survived and reorganised their lives despite adversity and this is what Rogers meant by our innate capacity to survive, grow and continue striving to reach our full potential.

In Rogers's theory, the organismic valuing process (OVP) sounds a little cumbersome but refers to our continually evaluating our own subjective experiences to see what possible impact they will have on our self-improvement.

FORMATION OF SELF-CONCEPT

The second most important part of Rogers's theory is based on the formation of the self. The self-concept refers to how we see ourselves and the world: The self is the sum of all of a person's experiences at any given time. An individual's sense of self develops as a result of their interactions with other people and their view of themselves. This means that people's perceptions of their individual selves are the organised set of characteristics that the individual perceives they have that are unique to them. Put another, more obvious way, our self-perception is how we see ourselves. Other people see us differently than we see ourselves; they see us from their perspective and how they experience us. According to Rogers, the self-concept is made up of conditions of worth and introjections; these are beliefs and values we hold but may be internalised from external sources, from our primary caregivers, our parents, teachers and friendship groups during our childhood.[7]

CONDITIONS OF WORTH

Examining childhood experiences in psychological ill-health in adulthood helps us to gain an understanding theoretically and to design and develop the appropriate therapeutic support – it is not intended to find blame or culpability in parents or caregivers. Generally, people behave in ways that they believe are right for them. They act according to their values and beliefs, just as Rogers claimed over 50 years ago. Humanistic psychologists taught us that for all people basic needs such as food, shelter, love and belonging are needed for our survival. Yet, we are unique as individuals, and we have unique life experiences, different families, upbringings and so on. Our development from a child to an adult is influenced by many different things, events, experiences, environmental situations and people in our social network.

The need for love and acceptance is strong and universal in human beings.[8] As children, we might learn that some behaviours are not acceptable in our home or in school, but children learn how to adapt to their environment. Take, for example, a young child who falls over and cuts their knee and begins to cry. An older adult, may say, 'you're fine, stop crying, don't make a fuss' and the child may internalise this response that it is not okay to express feelings, that it is wrong to cry, maybe crying is a sign of weakness, and that they should be 'strong.' It is unlikely that one incident like this will result in that message being internalised at that point. But if, on repeated occasions, a child learns not to express their feelings when upset, the child internalises the value or belief of the person who is setting the conditions on how to behave. Internalisation of another person's beliefs or values are introjected into the child's developing self-concept. The child then learns that they need to behave in a way that is acceptable to others, to 'fit in,' to deny their own experiences to comply with the adults' norms and values in the home or in their social network.

From observations in his therapy practice, Rogers claimed the cause of dis-ease or psychological distress and psychological ill-health in adulthood was due to people living their lives with introjected values and so denying their own true feelings. Introjected values play an important part in the developing self-concept of children in that there is a discrepancy between the self (with the introjected values) and their authentic self (their own values) and the person they would like to be (ideal self). The beliefs of others become introjected over time, and the beliefs and values from external sources are internalised as their own. Rogers also believed that we hold on to the introjected values in adulthood. The self-concept relates to our perceptions of ourselves and who we think we are. The discrepancy between who we believe we are and who we should be (how others expect us to be) results in 'incongruence,' a state of disjointedness: We are at odds with who we really are. Yet, some people behave in specific ways so that they feel accepted by others but, in doing so, they deny their own beliefs and values. We may not be conscious of our introjected values until we go to therapy.

PERSON-CENTRED THERAPY IN PRACTICE

Rogers, who initially worked in therapeutic settings with children before turning his attention to adults, saw the importance of creating a space for people to talk about their troubles. He was resolute in his belief that people needed to be listened to and understood so that they could grow as human beings and have their experiences validated and acknowledged. The relationship with the therapist provided the opportunity for clients to discuss and explore their issues and lives in the therapy room. The aim of person-centred therapy is to enhance the client's self-awareness and insight.

Person-centred counselling is a relational therapy.[9] People who have experienced difficulties in their interpersonal relationships, past or present, whose views and experiences have been ignored or denied, can address these issues within the safe and accepting environment with the person-centred counsellor. Person-centred counselling does not rely on techniques or interventions; instead, it is the therapeutic relationship that provides the healing environment for the client's experiences to be validated and the space for the client to grow and develop and experience a new sense of self.

THE ROLE OF THE PERSON-CENTRED COUNSELLOR

It is fundamental to Rogers's theory of therapy that therapists must be able to form experiential relationships with their clients, rather than being closed behind a professional façade. Rogers emphasised that this capacity to be with the client was as a result of the therapist's personal development and engagement in growth promoting activities, such as group and personal therapy. This 'way of being' is not developed by training or academic qualifications, although he acknowledged that training and qualifications were important.[10]

Influenced by the humanistic ideology, Rogers believed in providing a safe space to listen attentively to people's stories of who they are, who they were and who they would like to become. Based on the premise that therapy cannot be 'done' to, or on, someone, the role of the person-centred therapist is to provide a safe space, to listen without judgement, to be genuine and sincere in the relationship. This way of working has been considered as non-directive, although the term non-directive has stimulated debate in the literature in recent years.[11] Arguably, the mere presence of another person who bears witness to another person's story, can be directive. Person-centred therapy has been called person-centred, client-centred and even Rogerian. For Rogers, it was the therapeutic relationship between the therapist and the client that was the catalyst for change. People are just what they are right now, in the here and now.[12] The therapeutic relationship is an open, honest transparent interaction between the therapist and the client, there are no techniques or methods, or interventions to reduce symptoms or ease anxieties; rather, the focus is on listening to the client, validating their experiences by providing core conditions of empathy, respect and unconditional positive regard.

THE THERAPEUTIC RELATIONSHIP

It is clear that the attitude of the therapist is paramount in the person-centred approach. The therapist must be able and willing to sit with uncertainty, unknowing and free from the application of techniques. In this way, they can develop the attitude of unconditional positive regard and be non-judgemental about a client's behaviour or actions, to accept them as they are, present in the therapy room. Rogers stressed the importance of empathy, being able to see things from the client's perspective, to enter into the client's frame of reference.[13] The therapeutic relationship is important for other counselling approaches but not directly influential for a successful outcome. A warm sincere therapeutic relationship is more likely to build trust and help clients to buy in (compliance) to a model of therapy, for example, in cognitive behavioural therapy (Chapter 4) and positive psychotherapy (Chapter 5). Psychoanalysis places a high emphasis on therapeutic relationships, which manifests in countertransference and transference, but in a different way from the person-centred approach. In psychoanalysis, the therapeutic relationship is a method, an intervention, a way for a client to release inner turmoil and tension and to process old conflicts. In person-centred therapy, the therapeutic relationship is the crucial factor in helping the client change and become their true self. The relationship is considered to be the therapy.[14]

THE CLIENT IS THE EXPERT

Rogers believed the client is the expert on issues in their own lives. The client has the capacity for self-awareness to look for undiscovered meaning and purpose and direction in their lives if given the right environment to discuss issues of concern. Rogers believed that all of us have the innate ability to reach our full potential, to be the best that we can be, given the right circumstances and conditions.

> [I]t is the client who knows what hurts, what directions to go, what problems are crucial, and what experiences have been deeply buried. It began to occur to me that unless I needed to demonstrate my own cleverness and learning, I would do better to rely upon the client for the direction of movement in the process.[15]

THE SIX NECESSARY AND SUFFICIENT CONDITIONS

Three conditions underlie the therapeutic relationship in person-centred counselling: unconditional positive regard (acceptance); empathy and authenticity on the part of the therapist. For Rogers, the core conditions (the three core conditions) were necessary and sufficient to bring about change in a person's sense of self.

An interpretation of a client's experience was not necessary, as Freud suggested. The client is the expert, not the therapist. Originally, Rogers called his approach non-directive counselling, as the person-centred counsellor did not do anything to the client. There were no interpretations or techniques in this approach as seen in psychoanalysis. Rogers stopped using the term non-directive as he realised that the mere presence of one person impacts the other person.

Rogers believed that six conditions were necessary and sufficient for a client to grow, develop and change. Three of the conditions were related to the role of the therapist. The focus especially was on the quality of the relationship between the therapist and the client.

Here are the six conditions: (Adapted from Merry, 2020)[16]

Condition 1 – psychological contact between the client and the therapist. The client and the therapist need to have some psychological connection to participate in the process. This is sometimes referred to as a pre-condition for person-centred counselling. If this is not present, then the remaining five conditions are futile. Psychological contact in this regard means that the client and the therapist are aware of each other and of the potential impact of each other's presence during the therapy.

Condition 2 – the client's incongruence. The client is in a state of incongruence, which means a state of emotional distress and discomfort, or maybe has feelings of anger. Incongruence refers to a disconnect between awareness of underlying emotions and expressing those feelings.

Condition 3 – the therapist's congruence. This relates to the feelings and awareness of the therapist in the relationship. The therapist is aware of their own feelings and, if appropriate, may share those feelings with a client, but only if the therapist considers sharing their feelings to be beneficial to the client. The therapist is genuine. They can communicate openly and honestly what they're hearing and feeling. It is essential for a counsellor to be genuine and to communicate authentically.

Condition 4 – the therapist has unconditional positive regard for the client. The client does not have behave in a way to earn acceptance. There are no conditions in which the client has to present their best self for the therapist to like or accept them. Unconditional positive regard is also known as acceptance, and the counsellor accepts the client just as they are.

Condition 5 – the therapist's empathic understanding. This refers to the therapist's ability to show the client that they are trying to get a sense of who the client is and how they are experiencing their life. To enter the client's frame of reference, that is, to see things from the client's perspective and not the therapist's own.

Condition 6 – The client's perception of the client's conditions. The client must experience acceptance and warmth. As Joseph claims, if the client *feels* understood, he is understood.[17]

Rogers believed that these three core conditions (3, 4 and 5) create the environment for clients to explore their situations without fear of judgement or criticism. Rogers believed that if these six conditions were met, constructive personality change would occur, but only if all six were present. Rogers aimed at creating a growth-promoting environment, a safe space.

FULLY FUNCTIONING PERSON

So, if there are no methods or techniques, what would a client hope to gain from person-centred therapy? In 1961 Rogers developed a theory of what it means to be fully functioning. He described a client who emerges from person-centred therapy as a fully functioning individual, open to new experiences, with enhanced meaning in their lives, creative and ever-developing. Being true to themselves, being congruent, at ease with their own beliefs and values, recognising that they are always *becoming*; put simply, we are a work in progress.[18] According to Rogers's view of human development, person-centred therapy focuses on a client's personal meaning, which is a lifelong process. It does not aim to reduce symptoms of anxiety or depression.

A person-centred approach focuses on the quality of the relationship, the therapist providing the safe environment to facilitate the growth and development of the clients and heal psychological pain and distress. Thus, the therapeutic environment, according to Rogers, provides the client with a safe space to disclose their issue, or problems in living. Whilst trust between the therapist and a client is paramount in every therapeutic approach, it is fundamental in person-centred therapy. Rogers illustrated this in the core conditions. Person-centred therapy is not goal oriented, or time limited like we will see in CBT chapter 4. Instead, this approach is very much client-centred, where the client is not only the expert in their issues and their life but also in the duration of the therapy.

CRITICISMS OF PERSON-CENTRED THERAPY

Rogers made a rather bold statement that says that the core conditions are all that is needed for change within a client, regardless of the therapeutic approach. Not everyone agrees. As we have seen with in chapter 2 Freud's original theories were revised and modified by others – this is not unusual in the counselling field. Person centred therapy has evolved over time. Rogers original theories have been challenged by others. The issue of non-directivity is often debated and while many well-respected person-centred theories and practitioners believe the six conditions put forward by Rogers were necessary, they question the claim that that core conditions are sufficient to bring about change in clients. As a result, a 'family' or 'tribes' of person-centred approaches have emerged.[19] These alternative approaches (distinct from Rogers's classical person-centred approach) include Focusing by Eugene Gendlin, Person-centred and Experiential Therapies edited by Paul Wilkins, Learning Emotion-Focused Therapy by Greenberg, Elliott and Goldman and Existentially Informed Person-Centred Therapy Experiential – Counselling for Depression (PCE-CFD). We can't discuss each one of these approaches here, but if you'd like to know more about them you'll find links in the further reading and web resources section in this book.

CONTRIBUTIONS OF A PERSON-CENTRED APPROACH

Rogers's legacy is enormous. Not only did he revolutionise talk therapy from the 1940s to the present day, his theory and approach has wide applications. For example, client-centred therapy underwent a name change to person-centred to education, nursing, groups and conflict resolution. Like other influential thinkers in psychology, Rogers's ideas have become a part of daily life in our dealings and communications with each other. Treating people with respect, having an empathic understanding for others, considering what life might be like for someone else, compassion and being non-judgemental, particularly when encountering difference in others, are key to interpersonal relationships at home, in the workplace and in society in general.[20]

CONCLUSIONS

The person-centred approach to therapy is based on the idea that each person has innate capacities for self-understanding and to direct their own course of action. These capacities can be explored and developed within the therapeutic relationship. It also incorporates the view that all humans are essentially good, trustworthy and striving to become fully functioning individuals. Person-centred counselling is not goal driven: The aim of this approach is to help the individual fulfil their own potential, become a fully functioning individual, developing their sense of self, becoming the best they can be. In other words, achieving the self-actualising tendency, being open to experiences, having a sense of autonomy and independence from others' approval. According to person-centred theory and practice, clients do not need a therapist's expertise in method or intervention, as they themselves, the clients, are the experts on their own lives. The aim of person-centred therapy is enhancing the clients' understanding of their self, self-awareness and insight. This humanistic growth-promoting, positive approach to therapy was a forerunner to positive psychology and positive psychotherapy, which we will look at in Chapter 5.

NOTES

1 Schultz and Schultz (2015)
2 Maslow (1943)
3 McLeod (2013)
4 Kirschenbaum (2007)
5 Hergenhahn (1994)

6 Rogers (1963a, p. 6)
7 Claringbull (2010)
8 Claringbull (2010)
9 Mearns and Cooper (2017)
10 Hergenhahn (1994)
11 Sanders (2013)
12 Rogers (1961)
13 Rogers (1963b)
14 Joseph (2015)
15 Rogers (1961, pp. 11–12)
16 Merry (2020)
17 Joseph (2015)
18 Rogers (1961)
19 Sanders (2022)
20 McLeod (2013)

4

COGNITIVE BEHAVIOURAL THERAPY

INTRODUCTION

Counselling and psychotherapy are all about change. Yet we are surrounded by things, situations and areas of our lives that we cannot change. For example, we cannot change our history or past experiences, the families we were born into, or our world. So, if we cannot change these things, why do we go to therapy to seek change? We are changing how we perceive and deal with things rather than changing the things themselves. Behaviour change happens when we change our perspective of a problem or learn to cope with an issue. In the previous chapter, we looked at Rogers's theory of human development. His view of counselling focused on developing insight, self-awareness and change in perspective on specific issues. Another change approach is cognitive behavioural therapy (CBT). Cognitive behavioural therapy is a psychological therapy for common mental health issues and conditions such as depression and anxiety and complex conditions such as post-traumatic stress disorder and obsessive-compulsive disorder. Let us start with a brief background on the founders of CBT and then look at CBT in practice. In Chapter 7, Research in Counselling and Psychotherapy, we will look at the evidence that supports CBT as an effective psychological therapy.

DOI: 10.4324/9781003196471-4

BACKGROUND TO COGNITIVE BEHAVIOURAL THERAPY

CBT has its roots in the psychology and the work of early researchers: In behaviourism, that was John B. Watson (1878–1958) and B.F. Skinner (1904–1990), founder of operant reinforcement conditioning. Their work was supported by Joseph Wolpe (1915–1997), founder of Systematic Desensitisation for treating Post-Traumatic Stress Disorder. As noted in Chapter 1, Skinner and Wolpe are credited with the beginning of behavioural therapy in the 1950s.[1]

As we've seen, the increased need for talk therapies was due to social change and the expansion of psychoanalysis. Freud is credited with making therapy accessible for everyone – not only the middle classes or people categorised medically as insane. Albert Ellis (1913–2007) became disillusioned with psychoanalysis and, based on his experiences of his childhood loneliness and neglect, believed that unrealistic expectations fuel human misery. According to Ellis, how people think about themselves or events influences their emotional responses. He believed that some thoughts are irrational, and the client needs to challenge those thoughts to change the emotional response. Ellis identified rules for living and argued that people have 'crooked thinking' and live life with a fixed set of rules, such as 'shoulds and musts.' For example, 'everyone must like me and give me what I need' or 'If someone doesn't love me, they must hate me.' Ellis believed this exaggerated way of thinking was the actual cause of human misery and disappointment.[2]

Behavioural therapy extended to incorporate cognitive therapy, pioneered by Albert Ellis and Aaron Beck. Aaron Beck (1921–2021) is recognised as the father of cognitive therapy and developed ideas similar to Ellis. Cognitive therapy works by replacing self-defeating beliefs and behaviours with beliefs that focus on self-acceptance and problem-solving. The idea is that behaviour change is associated with emotions and cognitions. The Beck Institute and the Albert Ellis Institute websites have useful information on these two pioneers' work their theories' and biographical details. The combination of cognitive and behavioural therapies was announced in the publication *Cognitive-Behavioural Modifications: An Integrated Approach* by Donal Meichenbaum, and the new, technique-driven therapy CBT was born.[3]

We know that counselling and psychological therapies are influenced by social and cultural change and are generally accepted in society while also highly successful in helping people with real problems. Currently, CBT is one of the most popular and sought-after therapies for both common and complex mental health issues.[4]

COGNITIVE BEHAVIOURAL THERAPY IN THEORY

CBT is seen as a family of psychological treatments that teach us to feel better by changing how we think and behave. It is a problem-solving, time-limited, highly structured psychoeducational therapeutic approach.[5] It's different from psychoanalytic therapy and Rogers's person-centred approach because CBT emphasises problem-solving in the here and now. There's no room for the unconscious drives that create inner turmoil and tensions Freud spoke about. Nor is there much (if any) recognition given to Rogers's argument about conditions of worth, or internalised adopted values in childhood, which he believed are responsible for people's distress in later life. CBT is goal-driven and teaches clients to identify, evaluate and respond to dysfunctional thoughts and beliefs.[6] CBT is about perspective-changing, reframing thoughts, identifying and learning to unlearn unhelpful thoughts and behavioural patterns.

This approach to alleviating problems and stress needs the client to actively participate in the therapy as they learn that thoughts, behaviours, emotional responses and physical symptoms interact in positive or negative outcomes. This disorder-focused, evidence-based approach involves using what previously was called 'homework' sessions. Like many others working with CBT, I prefer to use 'between-session tasks.'

There are specific steps in CBT, and we don't have the time to go into too much depth in this book. But we can talk about what happens at the first consultation – this is one of the key areas in the treatment, as it focuses on assessing the client's issues.

COGNITIVE BEHAVIOURAL THERAPY IN PRACTICE

As mentioned in Chapter 1, the role of a therapist differs depending on the approach that they use and their assumptions about human development. The cognitive behavioural therapist works in collaboration with a client, helping them make sense of their inner and external world, their patterns of thinking and behaving and their patterns of responding and reacting to specific events, situations or people. The therapist will detail the treatment process and explain the reasons for adopting particular techniques and interventions. It is argued that by explaining each step of the therapeutic model at each session, the client will not only learn more about the process and their involvement in it, but they will be more likely to buy into the model of therapy and complete the course of treatment to achieve their goals.[7] In CBT terms, this is referred to as socialising the client to the model of treatment. In Chapter 3, we saw that the therapeutic relationship is considered the agent of change for clients in person-centred therapy. However, the core conditions of acceptance, warmth and empathy emphasised by Carl Rogers are not confined to person-centred therapy only. Almost all therapists understand and adopt the core conditions in their approach, and cognitive behavioural therapists are no different. However, the therapeutic relationship is not the focus of CBT: The catalysts for change in CBT are the specific cognitive techniques and behavioural interventions and not the quality of the relationship between the therapist and the client. Cognitive behavioural therapists are respectful to their clients and their problems and can show that they are genuinely interested in helping them resolve their issues. This builds rapport and trust in therapeutic encounters, and all professional therapists believe in creating a non-judgemental, safe and trusting environment for their clients.

The first consultation – assessment

The first consultation with a cognitive behavioural therapist can take approximately one hour. The first session's focus is a thorough assessment and evaluation of the client's issue. In some cases, the assessment might take two sessions. The therapist will explain everything, including the CBT therapy model and the treatment's structure, frequency and duration. Unlike other therapeutic approaches, questions relating to family history and childhood experiences are not included in the CBT assessment. The evaluation aims to gather as much information about the onset and duration of the current difficulties to see if CBT is a suitable treatment and get an overview of the problem from the client's perspective. The assessment is summarised, and the presenting issue(s) are sometimes formatted as a problem list with the client.[8]

CBT case formulation

From here, the therapist can hypothesise (formulation) how the problem started and select the most appropriate CBT intervention to treat the presenting issue. The formulation in CBT is about developing a theory or a hypothesis about a possible cause and context of a client's presenting problem and on events or situations that maintain and exacerbate the problem. The therapist explores the client's inner beliefs, fixed views, rules for living, trigger events and conditions and self-talk. The formulation is reviewed on an ongoing basis during treatment. According to Beck, when we develop a formulation, we are trying to identify the belief behind the behaviour, behind this problem, and the focus of the problem from the client's perspective. The formulation will evolve throughout treatment, but CBT's generic formulation applies to all conditions, common or complex.[9]

CBT structure for each consultation

CBT is highly structured, and specific issues are addressed in each consultation. The therapist and the client work together and agree on realistic short-term and medium-term goals and ensure that the client understands the complexity of the cognitive and behavioural therapy model. The therapist will ask for feedback at regular intervals during each session to ensure that they have an accurate view of the client's thought processes and to check progress. Checking the client's motivation for treatment and understanding what is required in task completion is crucial for cognitive behavioural therapy.[10]

Agenda setting at the beginning of each consultation is essential because it ensures that the key issues are addressed and are not overlooked. The agenda usually includes a review from the last consultation, progress on between-session activities, reactions to completing activities, and how the client managed any difficulties they encountered. CBT encourages self-help – it teaches clients to learn new coping strategies to become their own therapist and use methods and techniques for future problems. CBT treatment concludes with a plan to manage potential setbacks post-treatment.

CBT FOR COMMON MENTAL HEALTH ISSUES

Depression is a mental health condition that can affect a person's thinking, energy, and behaviour. It can vary from mild to severe and can profoundly impact their personal, social and working lives. Depression is a prevalent condition, and it can affect anyone, irrespective of age, gender or background. While there is a range of psychological treatments available to treat depression, CBT is generally considered effective in reducing the symptoms.[11]

The therapist's role when working with a client with symptoms of depression is to identify the thoughts when the client is feeling most depressed. They also reveal the possible triggers, situations or events when feelings of low mood and other symptoms get worse. Clients might notice certain times when their mood is low, when they are alone, or engage in certain behaviours. At this point the therapist will ask a fundamental question: 'What was going through your mind at that time?' This question is designed to help clients identify their own automatic, underlying unhelpful thoughts. The therapist will teach people to pay special attention to their thoughts. Human beings have a default setting to focus on negative thoughts more readily than positive thoughts. People who experience depression tend to accept their negative thoughts as facts. The cognitive behavioural therapist questions and challenges the client's unhelpful distorted thoughts and explains that thoughts are just thoughts; they are not facts.

While CBT is primarily concerned with thoughts (cognitions), it is important to avoid assuming that CBT is about positive thinking because it is not. This therapy focuses on teaching a client how different forms of thinking – underlying and consistent, helpful and unhelpful thoughts – can change feelings and behaviours. Beck developed a model of understanding depression from a cognitive perspective, which he called a 'cognitive triad,' based on his theory of emotion. This means that clients with depressive symptoms or a clinical diagnosis of depression tend to focus their thinking in three areas. They have negative thoughts about themselves, the world and the future.[12]

Regarding their self-talk, they may think, 'I am no good at this,' or 'I never seem to get anything right.' Thoughts about the world may include 'nobody cares about me.' They may feel they face a bleak future and think, 'will this ever end?' Or 'things will never get better.' Beck had a conceptual model to demonstrate the links between each component and how they interact together.[13] People with depression tend to have negative views, and in Beck's model, connections are made between the three areas. The CBT therapist will help the client identify distressing thoughts and evaluate realistic thoughts; they learn to change what we call 'distorted thinking.' The emphasis in CBT is on problem-solving and behavioural change to help clients adopt more helpful rational thoughts to feel better.

DISTORTED THOUGHTS AND THINKING ERRORS

Distorted thoughts, or 'thinking errors,' are common enough and are categorised in the CBT model as 'emotional reasoning,' 'all or nothing thinking,' 'catastrophising,' 'labelling,' 'mental filter' and 'mind-reading.'[14]

Let's start at the top. Emotional reasoning is when you think something is true because it feels true. All or nothing thinking relates to polarised thinking about an event or situation. In other words, you can only see two ways to think about things, good or bad. For example, 'I always get things wrong.' Catastrophising is a tendency to describe or think about something in the most extreme way, blowing the extent of an issue or problem up and out of proportion. For example, 'this will never stop' or 'I will never get another job.' Labelling is another thinking error we often see with clients when they label themselves negatively, such as 'I'm useless, a total failure.' A mental filter is a thinking error that refers to paying greater attention to negative detail instead of looking at the bigger picture. For example, at a work appraisal, your manager may have plenty of positive things to say about your work, compliments you on your commitment and dedication, but suggests a minor change to some work practices and room for improvement. With a mental filter, the client focuses only on the negative comment and interprets it to make them feel they are no good at their job. Mind reading is a type of thinking based on the belief that you know what others think, without question, without considering other possibilities.

Overgeneralisation is a distorted way of thinking where people tend to make general negative sweeping statements about themselves and their lives. An example of this might be that you wave at a friend across the street, and they don't wave back or acknowledge you. You may feel upset and hurt because you think that they ignored you. What you didn't do is think there might be another reason: They simply didn't see you. Or perhaps that other person has problems you are unaware of and were distracted.

An example of this is following a relationship breakup; someone might think, 'no one will ever love me again; I am unlovable.' These thoughts are limiting and fail to consider a future with possibilities and opportunities to find love again. 'Should' and 'must' statements – Albert Ellis has written extensively about shoulds and musts. He argued that it is people's expectations that cause misery and suffering. For example, the expectation that everyone must like you and that you must like everyone is unrealistic. CBT helps to work with clients to identify their fixed ideas about themselves and others. We often find that people have unusual, fixed ideas about themselves and others, often referred to as rules for living. For example, 'I should never make a mistake. I must be perfect.' The following quotations, dating back many centuries, simplify the basis of the cognitive aspect of CBT: 'People are disturbed not by events, but by the view they take of them,' 'Our life is what our thoughts make it,' 'It is not the situations in our lives that cause distress, but rather our interpretations of those situations.'

CBT interventions to change negative cognitions in depression include cognitive restructuring to identify and understand an individual's thought patterns (distorted thinking), activity scheduling, keeping a record of negative thoughts (thought journaling) and mindful meditation.[15]

SOCRATIC QUESTIONING

Training to become a CBT therapist is both extensive and specialised. Therapists are skilled at using and asking questions, using Socratic questioning. This was named after the Greek philosopher Socrates, who repeatedly asked questions to clarify meaning. Socratic questioning in CBT is a series of challenging questions to guide clients toward their treatment goals. This type of questioning is used to challenge thoughts, elicit emotion and gradually create insight or explore alternative actions (guided discovery). A therapist will ask specific questions to help identify the clients' thoughts and the situational context.

Here are some examples of Socratic questioning a therapist might use with a client who has depression and they are talking about a recent episode of low mood. 'What were you thinking at that particular time? Where were you at the time? What were you doing? Who were you with? Was there anything that made you feel better or worse?' The therapist's skill is to ask the questions in a tone that does not sound like an interrogation.

ANXIETY

Anxiety is a general term to explain frequent, unpleasant feelings of apprehension, dread or worry. Like depression, anxiety is a common condition that anyone of any age, gender or background can experience, and it's common for people to present with both depression and anxiety. Anxiety and depression are prevalent and recurrent problems and are significant causes of disability worldwide. There are several techniques and strategies for treating depression and anxiety. CBT treatment for anxiety follows the same protocol as the first consultation. However, the techniques for anxiety may be different, depending on the client. In agreement with the client, the therapist will offer the most appropriate one best suited to the individual client. Psychoeducation plays a vital role in treating anxiety (as it does in all other conditions): Explaining the symptoms and physical bodily reactions of anxiety aims to help clients understand the biological aspect of what happens when confronted with an anxious situation or an isolated panic attack. It is essential to find out about the situations that trigger anxiety and avoid them. CBT treatment for anxiety can involve cognitive or behavioural interventions.

THE VICIOUS CYCLE OF ANXIETY

Symptoms of anxiety are both unpleasant and frightening. Physical feelings, such as increased heartbeat, sweating and feeling nauseous or dizzy, can feel catastrophic or even like a heart attack for someone

with anxiety. The role of the cognitive behavioural therapist is to identify the client's thoughts when they are going through isolated events
of anxiety, such as panic attacks or when feeling anxious generally.
With CBT, it's vital to find out what events might trigger feelings or
episodes of anxiety, what maintains the problem and what keeps it
going for that client. It is also essential to determine the emotional
and physical responses at a specific time and other types of behaviours, such as meditating, checking, seeking reassurance and safety
behaviours when anxious. Clients may be asked to recall a recent
event or situation when feeling anxious, including 'what were your
thoughts at that time? What were your physical reactions? What did
you do?' CBT interventions for anxiety include cognitive restructuring, thought journaling, exposure therapy, activity scheduling and
behavioural activation. If you're training to become a CBT therapist,
rest assured you'll be supported by many treatment manuals for specific disorders, including depression, anxiety, substance abuse and
obesity. You'll also find the principles of CBT routinely used in self-
help books.

CBT – BECOME YOUR OWN THERAPIST

The overall goal of CBT is for each client to become their own therapist. CBT teaches clients strategies and techniques to help them cope
with their current and future problems. Christine Padesky, an inter-
nationally acclaimed therapist, has written extensively about CBT. Her
book (with Denis Greenberger), Mind Over Mood, is packed with helpful
self-help exercises for clients to use in their everyday lives. Padesky
argues that 'we are in business to put ourselves out of business, that
should be a therapist's goal.'[16]

DEVELOPMENTS AND FUTURE DIRECTIONS

Like all approaches, cognitive behavioural therapy has evolved to suit
clients' changing needs and in wider society. Researchers at the Beck
Institute are at the forefront of the broader recovery movement that

focuses on clients living meaningful lives. The latest development, called 'recovery oriented cognitive therapy' (CT-R), is a treatment approach designed to promote empowerment, recovery and resiliency in individuals with severe mental health conditions. CT-R aims to identify an individual's life goals and introduce strategies to help them achieve them. An individual with a complex mental illness can benefit from recovery oriented cognitive therapy (CT-R). It is a treatment approach that promotes empowerment relative to the challenges of the client's issues and symptoms. CT-R is grounded in the idea that everyone is capable of recovery, regardless of the severity of the condition. This new treatment moves from the traditional 'deficit model' of the human condition to a more 'strengths-based' approach.

Acceptance and commitment therapy

The 'third wave' of CBT refers to an expansion of CBT in the development of other therapies, such as 'acceptance and commitment therapy (ACT) and 'dialectical behavioural analysis' (DBT). ACT, pronounced as a single word, was developed by Steven Hayes in 2004.[17] It is derived from a philosophical position of grounded contextualism, focusing on language and its use. Techniques in ACT for the treatment of human unhappiness and distress are in stark contrast to those used in CBT. CBT can involve replacing, repairing, or removing faulty thinking, which fails to consider language and context according to Hayes and his colleagues. ACT aims to change the relationship a person has with their thoughts. ACT therapists do this by using a number of exercises to develop what Hayes calls 'psychological flexibility.' This approach focuses on strength, resilience and language, especially judgemental or self-critical language. ACT uses lots of exercises and metaphors to help clients see how they create meaning in their activities and actions, become more accepting and focus on values. It can also help clients decide what is important in their lives and develop a sense of purpose and meaning while being open to experience and how to make life work for them. Several studies have shown the beneficial use of ACT in a wide range of conditions. ACT techniques are not confined to therapy, and their techniques and strategies have been widely used in business, health and pain management. ACT founder Steven Hayes has released a useful self-help publication, *Get Out of Your Mind and Into Your Life*,[18] which describes useful ACT strategies which can be used in everyday life.

Dialectical behavioural therapy

Marsha Linehan first developed dialectical behavioural analysis (DBT) to help people diagnosed with borderline personality disorder.[19] There are four key components of DBT, and they are all aimed at helping clients regulate their emotions. The treatment typically consists of weekly individual sessions plus weekly group sessions. The focus is to give clients the skills to manage situations or events that they quickly react to and usually find intolerable. This should help prevent an escalation to more significant problems. Clients are taught skills around regulating their emotions, accepting and managing difficult emotions, improving people skills for more stable relationships with others and creating a more stable sense of self. DBT has a solid evidence base for its effectiveness in treating borderline personality.

CONCLUSION

We have learned from this chapter that CBT is an active, directed, time-limited, highly structured psychological therapy. It is the most effective, widely used and highly respected talking therapy of the 21st century. Its focus is to challenge clients' negative and unhelpful dysfunctional thoughts and thus change and improve their emotional responses and behaviours. Common myths about CBT include that this form of therapy is like positive thinking, that there is an over-reliance on technique at the expense of a client's emotional life, a lack of appreciation for the client as a unique individual, it's a quick fix, easy and a catch-all therapy that works for everything. While there is compelling evidence that CBT is effective for depression and anxiety, it's not a panacea to cure every mental health issue. This therapy focuses primarily on reducing psychopathology, arguably the goal of any therapy for many people who experience common mental health problems, such as anxiety and depression. Useful questions to consider are – can we assume that reducing depressive and anxious symptomology improves confidence and quality and meaning in life? Does the absence or reduction of depression and anxiety automatically improve psychological well-being? Probably not. Although CBT has been shown to be beneficial for many people, traditionally, it is a disease model of therapy, focusing on symptom reduction. It would be worthwhile to consider a strengths-based model of therapy, to think of a 'what's strong' instead of a 'what's wrong' way of understanding and improving psychological well-being; in recent years, a different perspective on mental health emerged with a focus on wellness. 'Positive psychology' and 'positive psychotherapy' depart from disease models and terms such as psychopathology and shift to focusing on strengths and reliance to manage our emotional distress and psychological well-being. Positive psychotherapy emphasises increasing positive emotional states, connections to and being valued by others and living a meaningful life. Chapter 5 will introduce positive psychotherapy and examine how this approach works with those who seek our help.

NOTES

1 Schultz and Schultz (2015)
2 Ellis and Ellis (2011)
3 Meichenbaum (1977)
4 Beck and Beck (2020)
5 Beck and Beck (2020)
6 Kennerley et al. (2017)
7 Beck and Beck (2020)

 8 Kennerley et al. (2017)
 9 Beck and Beck (2020)
10 Kennerley et al. (2017)
11 Jayasekara et al. (2014)
12 Beck et al. (1987)
13 Kennerley et al. (2017)
14 Kennerley et al. (2017)
15 Beck and Beck (2020)
16 Greenberger et al. (2015)
17 Hayes et al. (2016)
18 Hayes and Smith (2005)
19 Lmft (2022)

5

THE PROMISE OF POSITIVE PSYCHOLOGY

INTRODUCTION

In previous chapters, we have looked at things like misery, human suffering, dysfunctional thoughts and faulty thinking to try to explain certain aspects of a disease model of human development. Although they are all negative terms, they can be treated with standard psychological therapies. We have seen that psychoanalytic, and CBT types of therapy tend to reduce symptoms of 'disorders' and help people develop coping skills to deal with further psychological distress. Now, let us look at 'positive psychotherapy,' a strengths-based approach and an alternative to our already reviewed disease-based methods. Positive psychotherapy is the practical application of positive psychology. Before we go too far into it, it is important to know that the concept of positive psychology is not new. As part of the humanistic psychology trend which emerged in the 1950s, emphasis was placed on the positive aspects of life, focusing on how to bring out what is good in people. Abraham Maslow, the humanistic psychologist, was interested in motivation and urged us to take a more positive approach to human development. He first used the term positive psychology in his book *Motivation and Human Personality*, published in 1954.[1] This chapter will look at positive psychotherapy based on Seligman's theory

DOI: 10.4324/9781003196471-5

of well-being and not Nossrat Peseschkian's positive psychotherapy, founded in Germany in 1968.[2]

BACKGROUND TO POSITIVE PSYCHOTHERAPY

Professor Seligman has had a long and distinguished career in psychology. The early part of his work focused on experimental research into depression and other concepts, such as 'learned helplessness.' We needed to consider the positive side of human development because he argued that there was too much focus on the negative side of human nature. Professor Seligman formally launched positive psychology in 1998 in his presidential address to the American Psychological Association, which aimed 'to steer psychology away from the darkness and toward the light.'[3] This was seen as a new branch of applied psychology, and it challenged academics and practitioners to move away from the negative and destructive side of human experience and to focus instead on human flourishing and happiness and to look at ways to understand and help people become the best they can be and to live meaningful and purposeful lives. The publication of the *Positive Psychology Journal* in 2000 was a turning point in this new branch of psychology. Here's how Seligman and Csikszentmihalyi defined positive psychology in the journal:

> The aim of positive psychology is to begin to catalyze a change in the focus of psychology from preoccupations only with repairing the worst things in life to also building positive qualities.[4]

Of course, new areas of research and practice in positive psychology followed. In the last two decades, the positive psychology movement has become increasingly popular with several followers and a widespread acknowledgement of the benefits of the practical application of the theory of well-being. We can see this in the development of positive psychology interventions (PPIs).[5] The Positive Psychology Centre at the University of Pennsylvania has a wealth of resources and information on the science behind authentic happiness and well-being. The centre was established to promote research, training and education. Psychologists at the centre believe that human beings possess immense potential, and their goal is 'the scientific study of optimal human functioning' to make more sense of the human condition.

POSITIVE PSYCHOLOGY IN THEORY

Mental health issues, such as depression and anxiety, are researched scientifically, and we consider everything from genetics and early life influences on drug treatments and psychological therapies. Seligman and other experts tell us that we are stigmatising human suffering even further by concentrating our research on these areas.[6] We can all accept that psychological pain and distress are everywhere around us – it is a part of the human condition – but we know that we, as human beings, experience a full range of emotions, good and bad.

Freud told us that the best we can do in life is not to be miserable. Does that mean that human happiness is the absence of misery? If the answer is yes, then that would mean that the best you can hope for is not to suffer. Proponents of contemporary positive psychology believe that this is absurd and that the absence of misery does not automatically mean the presence of happiness and fulfilment. They also believe that everyone can aspire to happiness and well-being. Seligman and his colleagues tell us about the key factors in life that make life worth living, how we can thrive and flourish, be the best we can be in the present, and strive to be our best selves in the future.[7] Positive psychology introduces a new language, instils hope and helps us adopt an optimistic attitude to live a life of purpose and meaning.

According to Seligman, mental health issues are not problems about the past or the present; they are distortions of the future.[8] Depression has to do with *what you think* the future will be about, while anxiety is *a fear of the future*. We human beings tend to focus on negatives – it is our default setting.[9] But we know from our colleagues in neuroscience about 'brain plasticity,'[10] our brains' ability to change and adapt to new experiences; this includes new learning during and following therapy. Positive psychology and positive psychotherapy are not about undoing appalling events, resolving unconscious conflict, or challenging or unravelling twisted or distorted thinking. Instead, the theory and practice of positive psychology are about shining a light on a person's strengths, innate resources and capabilities and helping them move forward in their lives by building on their strengths. It is also about encouraging them to be mindful of their internal and external resources and use them daily. According to Seligman's 'Theory of Authentic Happiness,'[11] several routes to happiness exist. Shortcuts like alcohol, drugs, chocolate, television, and loveless sex are some of the routes we choose, and they may induce momentary pleasure and positive emotions. People who study and practice positive psychology are not critical of quick ways to experience happiness. Still, they warn us that relying on these shortcuts can result in emptiness and a lack of meaning. That can lead to negative feelings of dissatisfaction and psychological dis-ease. These temporary shortcuts to happiness may be positive in the short run but negative in the long term.

A MOVE AWAY FROM WHAT'S WRONG TO WHAT'S RIGHT

Positive psychologists tell us that other psychological therapies fail to consider our natural positive resources and strengths because they only focus on reducing symptoms. There is a large body of evidence (see Chapter 7) on the effectiveness of CBT in reducing symptoms of various mental health disorders. Proponents of positive psychology and positive psychotherapy do not call for disengagement from psychological pain. Instead, they are saying we should try an approach that considers the client as an autonomous person who has the ability to focus on what is good in life and in their circumstances to alleviate and shift attention away from psychological pain and distress.

THE PERMA MODEL OF WELL-BEING

We have seen that positive psychology has opened a new way of thinking about the human condition and helping people find meaning in their lives. The focus of traditional psychology has been, and continues to be, on 'what's wrong.' Positive psychology is about 'what's strong.' Positive psychology is not just about using positive language to make us feel better: The cornerstone of well-being is the concept of flourishing. This is the absence of misery and the presence of key elements such as positive emotions, engagement, relationships, meaning and accomplishment. Or PERMA. 'There is compelling evidence to support the PERMA model in helping people live meaningful and purposeful lives.'[12]

POSITIVE EMOTIONS

It is generally accepted that everybody wants to feel good, but people have different capacities to experience positive emotions. Some are genetically predisposed to low mood, but that does not mean they cannot experience positive effects. In positive psychotherapy, the therapist teaches the client ways to increase and enhance positive emotional experiences, such as cultivating forgiveness about the past, being grateful for past and present experiences, savouring physical pleasures and mindfulness and building hope and optimism for the future, imagining a better future self. That means the therapy has a psychoeducational aspect to it.[13]

ENGAGEMENT

Actively engaging in a task is another important aspect of well-being. So too is applying skills and strengths in a focused way, where you become totally involved in the task to the exclusion of everything else around you. Mihaly Csikszentmihalyi called this being in a state of 'flow.'[14] The activity in itself is its reward; examples of this are being fully engaged in conversation, reading a book, listening to music or writing. Whatever the task, being fully engaged is being totally absorbed at the moment.

RELATIONSHIPS

We are social beings. We like being around other people and forming emotional bonds with them. Close relationships are fundamental to a sense of well-being. Spending time with close friends and family allows the development of warm and satisfying relationships and provides opportunities to enhance positive emotions, making us feel good. Relating to others and spending time with people we care about helps us to show empathy and understanding to someone who may be struggling with an issue in their life. Satisfying relationships give our own lives purpose and meaning and allow opportunities for acts of kindness and emotional and practical support when they are needed. Clients are also asked to reflect on their relationship with 'self' and engage with self-compassion rather than self-criticism.[15]

MEANING

Human beings are meaning-making animals. In other words, we all want to live a life with meaning and purpose. Doing things, tasks or projects that shift your focus and energy from your immediate day-to-day situation is a wonderful way to increase your sense of well-being. Positive psychologists call this 'doing something larger than yourself.' It can be a local or a global project, for example, giving your time and energy to a charity or volunteering for some other worthwhile cause. Getting involved with the community can shift your priorities and foster meaning and purpose in your life.[16]

ACCOMPLISHMENT

Working towards goals and gaining a sense of achievement and accomplishment is also important in positive mental health. Whether the task is big or small, taking pride in something you have completed will increase positive emotions and feelings of worth and competence. These concepts are straightforward to understand – positive psychotherapy can help clients redirect their focus towards what is good in their lives and pay attention to the role of positive emotions, engagement, relationships, meaning and accomplishment in creating a plan for their positive mental health and well-being. Research has shown us that each of these building blocks contributes to well-being.[17]

This approach aims to help people identify and harness their inner strengths to increase their well-being and live meaningful and purposeful lives.

CHARACTER STRENGTHS AND VIRTUES

To understand what we mean by character strengths, let us look at the 'Virtues in Action (VIA) Classification of Character Strengths and Virtues,' which is a straightforward way to categorise human strengths and virtues. In Chapter 1, we learned that the *Diagnostic and Statistical Manual of Mental Disorders* (DSM-5) gives us a checklist of symptoms for various mental health disorders. In contrast to this, the VIA classification gives us 'a framework to categorise cognitive, emotional, protective, and spiritual strengths and positive traits in people such as curiosity, kindness, perseverance, hope, gratitude and humility, courage, modesty, persistence, vitality, social intelligence, spirituality, leadership, and humour.'[18] Christopher Peterson and Martin Seligman developed the VIA classification. Both theorists engaged in the mammoth task of intensive research on historical figures, such as Confucius, Socrates and Freud, and articles from contemporary social science researchers. They wanted to identify the character strengths and virtues that work best in people's lives, and the result is this alternative extensive classification system. A signature strengths survey was subsequently developed to help people identify their key strengths or signature strength as described by positive psychology. It ranks a person's strengths and can help people discover or rediscover their internal resources, leading to increased self-awareness and self-knowledge. You will find the signature strengths survey online.

POSITIVE PSYCHOTHERAPY IN PRACTICE

Positive psychotherapy (PPT) is defined as: 'the clinical or therapeutic arm for positive psychology which integrates symptoms with strengths, risks with resources, weaknesses with values, and regrets with hopes, to understand the inherent complexities of human experience in a balanced way.'[19]

This approach builds upon an individual's internal resources and is based on Seligman's PERMA conceptualisation of well-being and character strengths. 'It's designed to help individuals identify and build on their strengths to enable them to thrive, help them lead meaningful lives, cultivate their best resources, their character strengths, demonstrate how they can play to their strengths, and enhance their experiences in love, work and play.'[20]

Positive psychotherapy – what's involved

Positive psychotherapy therapy (PPT) is a three-phase model of therapy comprising 14 sessions. Following an initial consultation, the client is introduced to the process of positive psychotherapy and the therapist's roles and responsibilities. The first four sessions will focus on identifying and thinking about the clients' strengths. A central idea in positive psychology is for practitioners to give up the notion of correcting weaknesses. Instead, we need to focus our attention on identifying an individual's signature strengths and help them learn how to use them in work, in relationships and beyond. The VIA signature strengths survey aims to shift attention away from psychological distress and build on strengths that can boost well-being when used in therapeutic settings. According to advocates of positive psychology, identifying and building positive character strengths is the road to the good life. Phase two consists of four sessions exploring positive and negative coping strategies and reappraising past experiences. There are six sessions in phase three, focusing on enhancing interpersonal relationships and pursuing meaning and purpose in life.[21]

THE FIRST SESSION

As with any therapy, PPT relies on a caring, collaborative relationship between the therapist and the client. This is how we foster trust and rapport, motivate clients and encourage their engagement in the process. In Chapter 4, we saw that assessment during the first session of CBT was crucial in identifying problems and trying to ascertain what, how and when a problem occurs to design a tailored treatment plan for that specific problem. In traditional therapy, an initial meeting with a therapist usually involves trying to understand the 'presenting issue' or the problem. In contrast, in PPT, clients are asked to introduce themselves through a real-life positive story by recalling and reflecting on an experience that ended well. It is an exercise designed to help identify the client's character strengths. Focusing on a positive introduction can also generate positive emotions and instil hope in the client, which may inspire clients to adopt a new perspective on their lives. Clients are also encouraged to keep a journal containing as many of their positive experiences as they can remember.[22]

PPT takes an entirely different approach to mainstream therapies. Each session starts with a brief relaxation exercise. This is in keeping with the philosophy of positive psychology because it creates a relaxing atmosphere and helps build rapport between the therapist and the client. The first consultation begins with the client and therapist agreeing on how they will work together to achieve the client's goals.

POSITIVE PSYCHOLOGY INTERVENTIONS

We know a great deal about the influence that gratitude, curiosity, forgiveness and optimism have on our well-being. Seligman and his team had developed practical, straightforward exercises, referred to in the literature as positive psychology interventions (PPIs), and the research to date supports their utility in working with clients.[23] Positive psychotherapy combines the theoretical framework we have just discussed with positive psychological interventions (PPIs) to help clients identify their strengths and build on them to manage problems in their lives. The PPIs are broadly associated with each concept of the PERMA model, positive emotions engagement, relationships, meaning and accomplishment.

As a general rule, PPT interventions do not try to eliminate sadness and anxiety because it is accepted that negative emotions (like sadness, fear and anger) may have an adaptive function in a person's life: For example, there are times when sadness and fear are appropriate responses to life events and situations. PPT helps clients identify their strengths and the exercises help them develop what Seligman and his colleagues call 'practical wisdom.'[24] People with practical wisdom can cope with challenging situations in many ways.

There are several PPT interventions, and while we cannot list them all here, I can give you an example of some of the work in positive psychotherapy. As mentioned previously, the concept of gratitude is important in this approach, and clients are encouraged to write a 'Gratitude Letter,' which is a letter of thanks to a person who has helped them in the past. They may even consider contacting the person directly to express their gratitude in person. Other exercises include 'Three Good Things' or 'Three Blessings,' which encourages people to record three good things that happened during the day and then later each night to describe what made these things happen. Being grateful for the good things in life and the people in your life is an effective way to quickly increase positive effects and other positive emotions.

Another exercise is a 'Better Version of Me,' which involves creating a plan based on the client's goals for self-improvement in any or all areas of health, work, relationships or creative or financial enterprises. This exercise is similar to a personal strategic plan, creating a better, or best possible, future self. The therapist provides structured guidance on creating the plan to help the client reflect on the parts of self they wish to change and the parts they want to strengthen.

An exercise designed to build a realistic and genuine sense of optimism and hope teaches clients that challenges are only temporary. This exercise involves the client working through a realistic appraisal of what has happened in the past (doors closed) and what can be changed to move forward in their lives (doors opened). The 'One Door Closes, Another Door Opens' exercise aims to challenge and change self-defeating and self-sabotaging ideas the client may have of responsibility and blame for adverse events in their lives.[25]

POSITIVE PSYCHOTHERAPY – IS IT FOR EVERYONE?

The positive aspects of positive psychotherapy can help us understand that therapy is not all about reducing negative clinical symptoms. It is also about learning to identify and use your strengths, skills and abilities to face challenges and improve your well-being. Positive psychotherapy methods are not suitable for everyone, and we should be careful when considering using them with a client. *The Positive Psychotherapy Clinicians Manual*, by Rashid and Seligman, published in 2018, offers good advice and guidance on this approach and session-by-session direction on introducing clients to the therapy.

POSITIVE PSYCHOTHERAPY – DOES IT WORK?

From decades of research, we can measure and identify what we all call misery. The emergence of positive psychology means that we can now apply scientific principles to measure and identify well-being. There is extensive research literature on positive psychology and the benefits of the interventions used in positive psychotherapy. Adopting a grateful mindset is associated with fewer psychological symptoms. Gratitude journals and positive emotions can help us build a repertoire of better coping skills. Nurturing strengths increases growth and wellness. Strengths can function as a buffer against mental ill health. Recalling positive memories plays a vital role in mood regulation.[26]

THE GLASS HALF FULL

Optimism is an important concept in physical and mental health, but how do you define optimism? Here is an attempt: Optimism is a predisposition to expect positive outcomes in any given situation,[27] with the caveat that unrealistic optimism in the face of adversity or threat is not helpful and could be dangerous. However you describe it, optimism is important to our well-being. There is extensive research on its role in physical and mental health, and this concept is a crucial aspect of well-being. Individuals who have high scores on measures of optimism have more satisfying relationships, better self-regulation and coping abilities, lower levels of burnout, better overall physical health, fewer sleep problems, a stronger immune system and perform better at work.[28]

POSITIVE PSYCHOTHERAPY AND OTHER APPROACHES

Carl Rogers, who we met in Chapter 3, was one of the first psychotherapists to view human beings as resilient, innately good and having an inherent capacity for what he called the 'actualizing tendency.' This concept explains our ability to keep going and move beyond our current difficulties and personal challenges to strive toward a happier life. According to Rogers, in the right therapeutic conditions, the client can realise their potential and become a fully functioning person, which would result in them being more open to new experiences and so on. The therapist's role is to accept the person (the client) as the person they are, irrespective of their behaviour or thoughts. This safe, accepting therapeutic space will help clients reflect and become their 'true self,' and change will happen naturally. Stephen Joseph makes interesting points about the utility of blending person-centred therapy and positive psychotherapy in his publication, Positive Therapy: Building Bridges Between Positive Psychology and Person-Centred Psychotherapy, published in 2015.[29]

More recently, (as noted in Chapter 4) theorists in cognitive therapy have developed a strengths-based approach to recovery-oriented cognitive therapy (CT-R). This therapy tries to help clients with severe mental health issues to develop skills to build resilience and empowerment and focus on activities that will contribute to them living meaningful lives.

Seligman and his team stress they do not dismiss or devalue the work of psychology in designing and developing therapeutic approaches to help people manage distress and emotional pain. They argue that it is important to understand all aspects, good and bad, of human nature. They invite practitioners from all approaches to consider implementing positive psychology interventions as supplementary techniques to their primary methods.

POSITIVE PSYCHOLOGY – WHAT IT IS NOT

While positive psychology and positive psychotherapy are based on the principles of genuine happiness and the theory of well-being, Seligman and his team stress that this is not a 'happyology' – an attitude that everything will be fine, or everything will work out or anything that resembles a notion of a 'happy ever after' perspective. Positive psychology is not about positive thinking, which Seligman claims is an 'armchair' activity. The PERMA theory of well-being is carefully evaluated. There is consistent evidence that building character strengths, such as optimism and hope, are beneficial for relieving distress and enhancing our well-being.[30]

CONCLUSIONS

This chapter taught us that positive psychotherapy is a strengths-based approach to understanding psychological well-being. It offers a radical departure from a disease-based model of human development. Although the focus is on 'what's strong' as opposed to 'what's wrong,' positive psychology is not a Pollyanna view of the human condition. Instead, the aim is to ensure that well-being and suffering are considered equally important in human development. Therapies that focus only on reducing symptoms tend to neglect and diminish the strengths and resources individuals have within themselves to deal with adversity and negative experiences in their lives. Positive psychology introduces a new language and a new way of considering human nature. It is not a paradigm shift but a shift to balance therapeutic attention to strengths instead of weakness and hope as opposed to despair. Seligman and his team have developed several positive psychology interventions (PPIs) that aim to identify and build character strengths, induce positive emotions and support the five elements of the PERMA well-being model. There is no suggestion in positive psychotherapy that other psychotherapies are negative, nor does it seek to replace well-established methods. Instead, PPT focuses on refocusing therapeutic practices rather than redesigning them entirely. We saw the similarity in focus behind Carl Rogers's person-centred counselling, which is a positive approach. Human beings are constantly striving to be their authentic self, their best self and are determined to reach their potential.

Adopting specific techniques or interventions from widely recognised therapies can be helpful in counselling and psychotherapy; positive psychology interventions could complement other methods, including person-centred and cognitive behavioural therapy as suited to an individual client. Indeed, positive psychology interventions could be considered within a pluralistic approach to counselling, which you will read more about in Chapter 8, Professional Issues in Counselling and Psychotherapy.

NOTES

1 Maslow (1943)
2 Peseschkian (1987)
3 Seligman (1999)
4 Seligman and Csikszentmihalyi (2000 p 5)
5 Rashid and Seligman (2018)
6 Seligman et al. (2005)
7 Rashid and Seligman (2018)
8 Rashid and Seligman (2018)
9 Baumeister et al. (2001)
10 Lillard and Erisir (2011)
11 Seligman (2004)
12 Rashid and Seligman (2018)
13 Rashid and Seligman (2018)

14 Csikszentmihalyi (2008)
15 Rashid and Seligman (2018)
16 Rashid and Seligman (2018)
17 Rashid and Seligman (2018)
18 Peterson and Seligman (2004)
19 Rashid and Seligman (2018, p. 3)
20 Rashid and Seligman (2018, p. 3)
21 Rashid and Seligman (2018)
22 Rashid and Seligman (2018)
23 Seligman et al. (2005)
24 Rashid and Seligman (2018)
25 Rashid and Seligman (2018)
26 Rashid and Seligman (2018)
27 Carver et al. (2010)
28 Rashid and Seligman (2018)
29 Joseph (2015)
30 Rashid and Seligman (2018)

6

THE HEALING SPACE – A CHANGING LANDSCAPE

INTRODUCTION

Therapy professionals work in a variety of settings, such as schools, workplaces, prisons, health care, and in private practice. In these settings, a counsellor meets with a client regularly, usually once a week or once a fortnight, in a private room, seated at a comfortable distance from one another, for 50–60 minutes. This chapter takes us away from traditional room-based therapy environments, by exploring two distinct counselling spaces – online counselling and outdoor counselling. We will examine the way each environment impacts the way counselling is provided. While both therapeutic spaces have advantages and disadvantages, they both extend the reach of therapeutic support to individuals in need. A discussion of the key developments in the field of online counselling and ecotherapy over the past two decades will also be provided.

ONLINE COUNSELLING – WHAT IS IT?

Having access to the Internet has given us all access to the world. People of all generations can communicate positively, for the most part, connect to social networks and interact regardless of their location.

DOI: 10.4324/9781003196471-6

In the digital age, the Internet has revolutionized the way in which people conduct their everyday lives, and this includes the way they access psychological support.

Online therapy is a broad term which includes multiple ways of connecting to a therapist. It is also referred to as remote counselling, virtual counselling, web/cyber counselling or e-therapy.[1] There are various forms of computer-mediated counselling, synchronous forms which involve the use of relay chat, where users hold a live one-to-one conversation with a therapist in a chat room. Moderated group chat is also common amongst young people, where group members interact online with each other with a therapist also present. This form of support is scheduled at regular intervals, usually weekly. Asynchronous forms of online support include email counselling, where emails are exchanged between counsellor and clients, with a pre-arranged schedule, for example, weekly email communication and an agreed return time from the counsellor, typically with 48 hours of receipt of client's email.[2]

Technological mediated counselling is not new. As an alternative to in-person, face-to- face therapy, online therapy been delivered in the United Kingdom and in Ireland since the 1990s. The first reported paid therapy session online took place in 1995.[3] Advancements in technology and demand for services, especially in recent years, has resulted in mental health practitioners and counsellors now having a well established presence online, and it is believed that this area will continue to grow.[4]

STRENGTHS OF ONLINE THERAPY

The advantages of online counselling seem fairly obvious, such as accessibility and flexibility. Online platforms can facilitate the expression of emotions more freely and allow clients to disclose painful experiences more readily than face-to-face interactions. Online therapy can be accessed by people who have mobility issues due to illness or pain conditions or individuals who live in remote areas where counselling is not readily available. It is argued that online counselling may appeal to clients who are looking for short-term counselling, seeking help for one issue or for those who are seeking time-limited support for help with mild to moderate distress.[5]

Online therapy is appealing to adolescents who are considered digital natives (those who have grown up in digital world) and who are proficient with technology.[6] Online therapy offers clients more autonomy and control over sessions. For clients with high levels of body shame and self-consciousness, online support is preferred to in-person therapy because the distance and space is regarded as necessary for the client to feel safe engaging in the therapy. Online therapy allows clients to be more relaxed and less inhibited in what they say. They may disclose personal information which they would not feel comfortable discussing in person with a therapist. This is termed the online disinhibition effect by Suler (2004).[7]

Limitations of online therapy

The wide range of available options for therapy online is not a 'catch all' for everyone. There are distinct disadvantages associated with therapy in a virtual space. There are practical concerns about disruption to service and signal loss. Obviously, not being physically present with a client means that a therapist can miss the subtle cues and body language of a client; without visual and auditory cues, client-counsellor communication is more likely to be misunderstood.[8] Some populations are not best served by online counselling. Online therapy may be inappropriate for clients who have paranoia, rigidity, avoidance traits and a history of abuse as a child. Critics of this approach argue that online counselling may compromise security and confidentiality of clients' records. It has also been argued that asynchronous communication (delayed response) increases a client's anxiety, leaving them wondering about why there is a delay in responses from a therapist. Suler (2004) called this phenomenon the 'black hole phenomenon,' a situation in which you initiate some action online and do not receive a response.[9]

ETHICAL CONSIDERATIONS

As with all therapy, working with clients online raises a number of ethical concerns. Clients and therapists need a private space to talk, to avoid disruption from other people. Online therapists need to use a password encrypted web platform for client's confidentiality and privacy, they need to ensure the safe storage and retrieval of client's records and they need to be technologically competent. The growth of online counselling has led to practice guidelines from professional organisations like the British Association of Counselling and Psychotherapy (BACP) and the Irish Association of Counselling and Psychotherapy (IACP). These include issues such as the speed and immediacy of responses for asynchronous counselling, as well as the importance of providing alternate means of communication in case of technological failure and security breaches on the Internet. It is recommended that therapists who wish to work online engage in further specialist training and become informed about the research in the field.[10] The International Society for Mental Health Online (ISMHO), the Online Therapy Institute and the Association for Counselling and Therapy Online (ACTO) are good places to start for guidance on online therapy.

COMPUTERISED THERAPY PROGRAMMES

Through the use of specialised software, computer-based therapy became available in recent years. Computerised cognitive-behavioural therapy (CCBT) is the most commonly used form for the treatment of anxiety and depression. The structured approach of CBT makes it particularly well-suited to IT. Ratings of symptom severity and distress are used to track therapy progress. An example of these programmes are: Fearfighter (www.fearfighter.com) and Beating the Blues (www.beatingtheblues.co.uk). Delivered online, the Fearfighter programme treats panic, anxiety and phobia. The course consists of 10 sessions with 4–5 hours of homework each week and a brief helpline support. Beating the Blues is a CBT interactive online programme for the treatment of depression, delivered over 8 sessions.

As the use of CBT for treatment is widely supported, there still remains the important question, is computerised counselling like CCBT as effective as traditional face-to-face interactions? The answer is – generally speaking, yes. Research shows that that CCBT achieves similar results as CBT delivered in a face-to-face context.[11] This evidence contradicts the long-held belief that the therapeutic relationship is crucial to therapy and positive outcomes.[12]

It is important to note that the CCBT is considered a form of self-help to assist the individual in establishing autonomy, engagement and motivation, which are all important elements of a successful treatment programme.[13] Some computer packages still retain the human involvement, with additional helpline support provided during the programme and some do not, as is the case in artificial intelligence for psychological support.

ARTIFICIAL INTELLIGENCE – COMPUTERS THAT CARE?

Artificial intelligence (AI) is science fact as opposed to science fiction.[14] While AI has received a lot of press in recent years, the use of AI in counselling is not new. As far back as 1956, Weizenbaum and his colleagues created an innovative computer program known as ELIZA. This is a text-based interactive service, based on Rogers's client-centred approach. Users of the service can type in their issue, disclose their personal feelings and thoughts and receive a response immediately. Eliza is still with us and ready to chat; she can be found at ELIZA.com.

Meet Tess, the virtual therapist (a chatbot). Tess is available 24 hours a day, seven days a week. The company, Ellie X2 AI founded by Michiel Rauwas, aims to provide affordable and on demand mental health support. Tess as introduced is advertised on the company's website as a mental health chatbot providing self-help chats, on demand. You might ask, how can a human therapist compete with that? In the corporeal world, counsellors are human and have other commitments and competing demands, such as work, family, sleep and so on. As a result, we are not always available to clients. However, it is unlikely that artificial intelligence will replace the need for human interaction between counsellors and clients. Although chatbots and carebots can be useful in providing additional support, AI cannot explore the subjective experience of clients in the same way as therapists can, regardless of how much technology aims to humanise their creations.

Online counselling is not currently included in core counselling training. As advancements in technology occur rapidly, educators and training providers in counselling need to keep up with these developments and incorporate various forms of cybercounselling into their curriculums. Notwithstanding ethical issues noted in computer-mediated counselling, software packages and AI, it is difficult to predict what the future holds for online counselling, and the magnitude of computerised programmes and AI in therapy remains unknown. However, it is reasonable to say that online counselling promises to play a greater role, either as stand-alone support or as part of an integrated blended model of therapy.

Since the Internet has become a valuable source of information, entertainment and communication, it's no wonder that health care has expanded to the cyber world in the form of e-therapy. While the obvious benefits of technologically mediated counselling are recognised, there are some challenges. Deciding to provide or to avail of online counselling, it is important for counsellors and clients to be aware that online counselling is not suitable for everyone. We now move to a very different counselling space, to therapy in the 'great outdoors' otherwise known as ecotherapy.

Green spaces – physical environment

Our emotional and general well-being are constantly impacted by our physical environment, even though we may be unaware of it. In traditional therapy the design and layout of counselling rooms can influence both the client and the therapist's experience. In office-based therapy practice, clients perceived sense of psychological and physical safety and their ability to disclose personal information can be influenced by the layout of the therapy room. While there is no single design that is conductive to a therapeutic room, colour, seating and windows to let sunlight in are key areas to take into consideration.

Previously, we examined counselling in the virtual world. The popularity and the benefits of online counselling were described. However, poor Internet connection can be troublesome, irritating and disruptive and changes the 'space' between the therapist and the client. We know that the environment in which we practice therapy, the 'healing space,' is important for both the client and the practitioner and influences the therapeutic experience for each person.[15] Despite the popularity of technologically mediated counselling, a counter-movement has emerged that is striving to acknowledge our relationship to nature. Ecopsychology and ecotherapy reminds us that we are organic, relational beings with deep connections to the natural world.[16]

ECOTHERAPY – WHAT IS IT?

Ecotherapy is a form of psychotherapy which includes the use of natural environments and materials to help improve mental health and psychological well-being. Although the term ecotherapy was first coined by Clinebell (1996), the concept of green therapy is well established and predates almost all of today's therapies. Throughout history, humanity has been viewed as integral to nature, with mutually beneficial relationships between both. As early as 1858, an appreciation for green spaces was acknowledged with the construction of New York's Central Park. Calvert Vaux and Frederick Law Olmsted designed the world famous 845-acre park to provide a peaceful recreational green space so inhabitants of the rapidly growing city could be immersed in nature. There are some counsellors who view ecotherapy as a three-party relationship between client, counsellor and nature, in which nature serves as a catalyst for healing; put another way, an appreciation of the natural world in therapy views nature as a co-therapist 'in the therapeutic relationship.'[17] Clinebell (1996) viewed ecotherapy from an ecological spiritual perspective, which considers both nature's ability to nurture us through our relationship with the natural environment and our ability to reciprocate this connection by nurturing it.

Ecotherapy interventions

In ecotherapy, interventions are mainly experienced outdoors in a green environment (but it can also be experienced indirectly indoors). Ecotherapy interventions include several diverse activities, including the following:

- In animal-assisted therapy a therapeutic relationship is formed with an animal, such as a horse or dog, known as equine or canine therapy.
- Walk and Talk therapy can be less intimidating than therapy indoors; it can help clients talk and relax more than in face-to-face interactions and it encourages present moment awareness.
- Wilderness Therapy – engaging in nature activities in remote areas.
- Animal assisted interventions involve direct contact with animals, for example, visiting a farm.
- Adventure therapy – taking part in adventurous physical activities in a group, such as abseiling, rafting, or hiking.
- Forest bathing or a leisurely walk in the woods – mindfully taking in the atmosphere, sights, sounds and aroma of the environment.
- Green exercise therapy – walking, running or cycling in green spaces.
- Nature-inspired arts and crafts – involves being creative, making art or crafts with natural materials such as wood, grass and clay.
- Taking part in social and therapeutic horticulture involves gardening or growing food, in allotments or community gardens.

Recent research has consistently shown how nature enhances various aspects of well-being.[18] While there are many different green activities to choose from, a simple walk in the park or taking time to observe the growth of plants or a visit to a beach or the sea has shown to lower stress for people with busy lives and living in urban towns and cities. It has been 20 years since green spaces have been the subject of intense research. There is increasing evidence supporting the health benefits of interacting with and viewing green space on psychological well-being such as depression, stress reduction and post-traumatic stress disorder.[19] We know that mental health may be improved by the presence of even small elements nature. It can be beneficial to have plants in the office, a view of a serene landscape, or access to a courtyard or garden nearby to enhance your therapeutic experience.

Ecotherapy – strengths

It is possible for practitioners to introduce or combine ecotherapy intervention concepts with established counselling theories as eco-therapy is not an independent modality.[20] Research in ecotherapy has shown that sensory experiences are important. When engaged while being outdoors, scents of natural environments, sounds of nature, water flowing, the visual aspect of looking at greenery and views of nature have a calming effect on our nervous system and a positive impact on mood. The restorative benefits of ecotherapy have been widely acknowledged.[21,22] Embracing the natural environment can lead to beneficial outcomes, as summarised next.

- Green exercise is physical activity undertaken in green and natural settings and is linked to positive mood and emotional well-being compared to exercising indoors.
- Viewing or being in close proximity to blue spaces, for example, coastal areas of lakes, are beneficial to psychological well-being.
- Walking in parks or forests has been linked to a reduction in stress levels.

Ecotherapy – limitations

There have been some criticisms of ecotherapeutic interventions despite increasing evidence of their efficacy.[23] There are practical and ethical concerns among practitioners that prevent their engagement with this approach, including: time constraints, boundary issues, confidentiality and legal concerns, unsuitable locations and insufficient awareness and confidence to implement certain activities.[24] Client preferences and suitability for therapy are also important factors to consider; some clients may not be comfortable taking therapy outdoors. Therapists and clients may perceive some techniques as having limited benefits because they are relatively easy to implement. It is likely that not all clients would be open to such a course of therapy, as some interventions, like hiking, or activities in wilderness therapy may cause discomfort. That said, there has been an increase in the popularity of ecotherapy in recent years, with many mental health services including a green agenda and receiving significant funding to implement ecotherapeutic interventions. Green prescribing began in the United Kingdom in 2020 in selected areas, but it is likely that this could become mainstream in the future, given a recent review which found that there is no evidence to support the claim that depression has a biochemical basis.[25] This will have implications for drug treatments for depression and calls into question the use of SSRs to treat the disorder. This finding may encourage more healthcare providers to consider green prescribing. This is where patients are advised to use exercise in the open air to improve their mental health and well-being. It can also include being prescribed walking, cycling or working with others in community gardens or a conservation project or joining a green gym. For more vulnerable populations, it could include supported visits to local green spaces or more structured ecotherapy interventions. It has been shown that spending time outdoors on a weekly basis is linked to better physical and mental health, as well as greater psychological well-being than those who do not spend time in nature.[26]

In summary, globalisation and a digital gadget culture have led to an increasing disconnect from nature, yet there are plenty of ways to stay connected and increase well-being. Ecotherapy techniques and interventions have enormous promise as a standalone approach or as an adjunct to another approach. Based on the principles of positive psychology outlined in Chapter 5 some ecotherapy interventions could be incorporated into positive psychotherapy to help clients flourish, build character strengths and to promote personal growth. Regardless of online or outdoor counselling, the aim of the therapy remains the same – the therapeutic space is the only thing that changes. For therapists interested in this approach, see Andy McGeeney's book *With Nature in Mind: The Ecotherapy Manual for Mental Health Professionals*, published in 2016.[27] This book provides practitioners with lots of useful, evidence-based techniques and guidance on how to facilitate effective and safe outdoor sessions with adults.

Conclusions

We considered two different spaces in counselling and psychotherapy, online and outdoors, each with strengths and limitations to consider before working with clients in either space. Online has much to offer to clients who are living in remote areas or for those who have mobility issues or a chronic illness that prevents travel to the therapist's office. Disruptions in online connections and the lack of personal qualities, in video, or email counselling that are experienced in face-to-face interactions limits the appeal of cybercounselling for some people. In contrast, ecotherapy techniques provide an opportunity for people to connect to the natural world and improve their well-being.

Interventions in ecotherapy take place primarily outdoors and range from simple walk and talk therapies to horticulture therapy, or wilderness therapy. However, ecotherapy does not focus exclusively on outdoor activities, and there are other ways to connect with nature, for example, through creative arts and crafts with natural materials, pet ownership or tending to plants indoors.

The simplicity of some ecotherapy interventions should not diminish their value; they can be transformative for some people's well-being. There is good evidence to support the effectiveness of this therapeutic approach in various physical and mental health issues.

The increasing awareness of mental health issues and well-being in the popular media and the Internet has increased the demand for therapy. As clients are consumers of counselling, it is important to consider their ideas or preferences in the way they would like to address their particular issue. No one approach or intervention is a cure for mental ill health or psychological pain or dis-ease. There are, however, many different approaches and techniques that reduce psychological distress, change behaviour and help people live meaningful lives and enjoy meaningful relationships with other people and with the natural world. The adoption of using different approaches to suit a client's particular need as opposed to adhering to a single orientation is a contentious yet an important debate in counselling and psychotherapy. In Chapter 8, we'll explore a pluralistic approach to counselling in greater detail. Now let's turn our attention to the research in counselling in Chapter 7 and find out if any of these approaches work.

NOTES

 1 Barker and Barker (2021)
 2 Barker et al. (2010)
 3 Hanley (2020)
 4 Hanley (2020)
 5 Barker and Barker (2021)
 6 Barker and Barker (2021)
 7 Suler (2004)
 8 Nagarajan and Yuvaraj (2021)
 9 Suler (2004)
10 Barker and Barker (2021)
11 Treanor et al. (2020)
12 Mearns and Cooper (2017)
13 Treanor et al. (2020)
14 Banks (2018)
15 Kamitsis and Simmonds (2017)
16 Chaudhury and Banerjee (2020)
17 Clinebell (1996)
18 Summers and Vivian (2018)
19 Summers and Vivian (2018)

20 Hanley (2020)
21 Coventry et al. (2021)
22 Walker et al. (2021)
23 Chaudhury and Banerjee (2020)
24 Chaudhury and Banerjee (2020)
25 Moncrieff et al. (2022)
26 White et al. (2019)
27 McGeeney (2016)

7

RESEARCH IN COUNSELLING AND PSYCHOTHERAPY

INTRODUCTION

In Chapter 1 we learned that counselling is effective for 80% of clients, that is 8 out of 10 clients will experience a positive outcome from therapy. What happens to the remaining 20%? This is the big question in counselling and psychotherapy. Five decades ago, Paul (1967) raised the question 'What treatment, by whom, is the most effective for this individual with that specific problem, and under what set of circumstances?'[1] The research agenda in counselling and psychotherapy has extended to include not only what treatment is effective, but also to other areas, such as the client's experience of the therapeutic process, investigating the influence of therapists' personality and characteristics on client outcomes. Yet some questions remain, such as do clients actually gain more from therapy than they would have without it? Is it possible for therapy to cause more harm than good? The scope of this book prevents me from discussing these issues in depth. However, I will discuss how we can confidently say that therapy works – for some people – why research in counselling and psychotherapy is important and highlight some important findings from decades of research in the field. In this chapter, you will be introduced to different ways in which we acquire knowledge which

DOI: 10.4324/9781003196471-7

will enable you to be a more critical consumer of knowledge, in the sense that you will be able evaluate how we arrive at the claims made by others, that we are presented with every day. Understanding the research process in counselling and psychotherapy can empower you to make informed decisions about talk therapy.

RESEARCH – WHAT IS IT?

The term research is derived from the middle French term 'recherche' which means 'to go about seeking.' In its simplest terms, research is about searching for knowledge. In a formal sense, research is defined as a systematic process of enquiry that leads to the development of new knowledge. Research is a natural day-to-day activity; before we do something or go somewhere, we do our research – we do this because we want to find out information, evaluate the information and make an informed decision. When we purchase an item like a phone, computer, car or house, we don't pick the first one we see; we look at many to find out key features about them and assess if they suit our needs. We take part in research activities every day. Yet the word 'research' seems rather harsh – it depicts an image, for some, of people in white coats in a laboratory. Research can take place in a laboratory, but it also takes place in lots of other settings.[2]

HOW DO WE KNOW WHAT WE KNOW?

If the purpose of research is to gain new knowledge, how can we trust the findings from new knowledge? This leads us, as consumers of research, to think about how we acquire knowledge. There are several ways in which we acquire knowledge; textbooks will often refer to these ways as methods to acquire knowledge and are further distinguished between scientific and non-scientific methods.

Non-scientific ways of acquiring knowledge are through methods of tenacity, intuition and authority. The scientific method is very detailed and it produces answers that we can share with confidence. Research uses the rules and principles of the scientific method to identify a problem, relevant data is gathered and at times a hypothesis is formulated (quantitative) and is then empirically tested. Qualitative research adopts a systematic approach and has rigorous procedures to collect and analyse data and present findings but in a different way to quantitative research. In both quantitative and qualitative research, data is analysed and conclusions are drawn and shared in the public domain, typically, though not exclusively, through publication in peer-reviewed journals.

Method of tenacity

Acquiring knowledge through tenacity refers to accepting information as true because it has always been believed or because it is supported by superstition.[3] This method of acquiring knowledge is based on habit. We continue to believe something because we have always believed it. For example, it is likely that you have heard that 'opposites attract' meaning that we are attracted to people who are different to use in terms of personality and so on. The more frequently we are exposed to statements like this, the more we believe them to be true. The method of tenacity is used every minute of every day by marketing and advertising companies and social media. Messages are repeated over and over again, leading us to believe they are true. Superstition also plays a part in the method of acquiring knowledge; everybody 'knows' Friday the 13th is unlucky. . . . Really? The problem with acquiring knowledge through the method of tenacity is that the information may not be accurate, as it is not grounded in evidence. Take, for example, opposites attract. Research in social psychology has consistently shown that this is a myth; we are attracted to people who are like us, and we pursue longer relationships with people who share the same beliefs and values, political views and certain aspects of intelligence.[4,5] Scientists have debunked some widely held beliefs about human behaviour, which Scott Lilienfeld and colleagues discuss in their book, 50 Great Myths of Popular Psychology (2009). Among them were 'People only use 10% of their brain.'

Method of intuition

Another way of knowing something is by relying on our intuition, our gut feelings, a sense that something is right or wrong. Being guided by intuition involves trusting your gut, rather than exploring the facts or reasoning to reach a conclusion about something. In this way, intuition involves *believing* what *feels* true. It is possible for our intuition to be wrong since our judgement can be prejudiced by our own biases and desires rather than logical reasoning or scientific evidence. We may use intuition or a 'hunch' to answer some questions and there is nothing wrong with this to make decisions about everyday situations, but the method of intuition would not be appropriate for serious situations that require careful consideration and deliberation such as when a therapist is deciding what may be the best therapy or method for a client. We use mental shortcuts, called heuristics in forming and maintaining believes. If a belief is widely shared, we are inclined to believe it, especially if the belief is endorsed by experts. Gravetter and Forzano (2011) claim that we tend to hold onto such beliefs because it would be nice if they were true.

The method of authority

As a common method of acquiring knowledge, authority involves accepting new ideas based on the statements of an authority figure. These authorities are parents, the media, therapists, doctors and lawyers. This is where a person finds answers by seeking out an authority on a topic or subject area. This can mean consulting an expert directly or going to a website to find out information to address an issue. In this case, you are relying on the assumed expertise of the person to answer your questions so you can make an informed decision on your issue. Relying on the method of authority, the person seeks guidance from an expert in the subject area. For many questions the method of authority is a good place to start; it is the easiest and quickest way to obtain answers. However, there are some drawbacks to using this method to acquire knowledge as information received by assumed experts in the area may not be accurate and may be biased. Authority figures should be trusted in an ideal world, but history has shown us otherwise, which has led to serious consequences.

We acquire most of our knowledge in our daily lives through authority, as we do not have the time to question everything we learn and examine every piece of information independently. But we can learn to be more discerning and learn to assess whether authority figures are credible. We can assess their methods of arriving at their conclusions, and to assess whether they have any motives to deceive or mislead. We must evaluate the methods they used to acquire their knowledge.[6]

Method of rationalism

Rationalism or reasoning is reaching a conclusion using a set of premises. Rationalism uses logic and reasoning to acquire new knowledge. In order to arrive at a good conclusion, a premise must be stated and logical rules must be followed. The problem with this is if the premise is wrong the conclusion drawn is wrong. For example, someone might say, 'All children like ice cream.' 'Alex is a 5-year-old child,' therefore 'Alex likes ice cream.' These broad generalisations are not always true.

Method of empiricism

This method involves acquiring knowledge through observation and experience. For example, you may believe that all swans are white; if so, this assumption comes from your experience. It is based on your personal experience of only ever seeing white swans, but black swans also exist and can be found in Australia and in New Zealand. There was a time people believed the world was flat because it appeared that way. These are just two examples of the limitations of our experiences and how we can acquire false information. That said, empiricism is at the core of the scientific method. Faith in this method is borne out in the phrase, 'I'll believe it when I see it,' which shows us how much faith we have in our own experiences.[7] But a note of caution, our perceptions are influenced by our past experiences, our beliefs and our emotions and they may not be always trustworthy; our perceptions can let us down. We can misinterpret what we see. What we observe and our perceptions are subjective. We each perceive the world differently, reflecting our own uniqueness. Philosopher Henry David Thoreau sums this up nicely, 'It's not what you look at that matters, it's what you see.'

The scientific method

If we cannot rely totally on our gut feelings, our experiences and observations, reasoning or the expertise of others, how can we know for sure that the claims made by psychologists and therapists on the effectiveness of therapeutic approaches are valid? The answer is science – science is one way of knowing about the world we live in. There are three goals of science – to describe, to predict and to explain.[8] In its broadest sense, science refers to any systematic process that aims to acquire knowledge. We make observations that can be measured as part of the scientific method. Empiricism and rationalism are the key components of the scientific method to determine the validity of conclusions reached.[9]

Outcome research in counselling and psychotherapy is based on the scientific method, relying on well-established rules and principles and the adoption of a standardised approach to gathering information, analysing data, reaching valid conclusions and publicly disseminating their findings. Research therefore is a process of systematically collecting and evaluating evidence to test ideas and answer questions. While scientists may use intuition, authority, rationalism and empiricism to generate new ideas, they don't limit themselves to these methods. In addition to systematic empiricism, scientists also make careful observations under conditions that can be controlled in order to gain insight into the phenomenon of interest. Their ideas are tested by rationalism and valid conclusions are reached. Students of counselling and consumers of therapy need to understand the importance of the scientific method in order to have confidence in the therapeutic process.

RESEARCH IN COUNSELLING – WHY DO WE NEED IT?

It has been my experience for years that students who enrol in my research methods course are apprehensive about research. There are many students who think that becoming a therapist is a great career (which it is), they are passionate about mastering clinical skills and learning different methods of therapy but they question why they have to enrol on research module, which they deem 'difficult' and a little boring. Most students, however, begin to lose their concerns about research as they move through the module and they begin to understand its importance in the field of counselling and psychotherapy. The change in their attitudes is largely brought about by their understanding of what research informed practice means and learning ways to gather information and answer questions so as to become better equipped to understand the utility of therapy and contributions to effective therapeutic experiences.

For counselling and psychotherapy, conducting research is necessary for a variety of reasons, including the need to establish and maintain the trust and confidence of the public by providing quality assurance to clients, maintaining the credibility of our practice of therapy, developing training that is of high quality and understanding and evaluating therapeutic process and outcomes. Research in the field allows us to differentiate between beneficial and harmful practices and it helps us to enhance practice and inform policy, strengthen our reputation and have a voice in an evidence-based work culture. Research can help us to review and modernise theories, and factors that might cause clients to change can be determined.

DIFFERENT RESEARCH APPROACHES FOR DIFFERENT QUESTIONS

It is argued that helping practitioners are natural researchers, and as such, all types of practitioners have a responsibility to add to the knowledge base of therapy. If we work from the premise that research is about adopting scientific principles to find the 'truth,' then we have to consider the definition of 'truth.' Researchers adopt different approaches to their studies, for example, adopting either a quantitative or qualitative approach or by adopting mixed methods research (blending both quantitative and qualitative). Although the research question determines the research approach, researchers hold different assumptions about what constitutes 'truth' in research. There are polarised views in the research community of what constitutes 'truth' in research. For example, quantitative researchers argue that truth is objective, something that is measured objectively. Researchers with this belief adopt a quantitative approach to research. An opposing view is held by those who believe that there is no objective truth, rather, that meaning of experience is socially constructed, and that 'truth' is subjective and therefore variable depending on perspective. Qualitative approaches are typically adopted to carry out process research. Studies in this area typically explore perspectives or subjective accounts of an experience or phenomenon. Qualitative research advances our knowledge of specific components of the therapeutic encounter, or of clients' experiences of therapy. Qualitative research in counselling gives voice to clients and therapists.[10]

RESEARCH IN THERAPY – THE STORY SO FAR

In Chapter 2 we learned that Sigmund Freud moved away from medicine to develop his own therapy called psychoanalysis. One of the criticisms of his approach was that there was no evidence to support Freud's claims about the unconscious drives and psychological ill health. While at the University of Chicago, Carl Rogers established a counselling centre to study his non-directive therapy, as it was called at the time. He is widely regarded as the first psychotherapist to conduct research in psychotherapy.[11] He published his findings in a book – *Client Centred Therapy* in 1951. He was honoured for his pioneering research with the Award for Distinguished Scientific Contributions by the American Psychological Association. There has been a vast amount of research published since Rogers's time. Researchers in cognitive and behavioural therapies have led and continue to lead in outcome research in psychotherapy. While person-centred research has significantly advanced our knowledge in process research, relatively little outcome research is conducted on this approach. It has been argued that counsellors have traditionally shown little interest in either conducting research or reviewing the literature.[12] Over the past two decades, the UK government has invested heavily in providing funding for therapies that were found to be effective, known as evidence-based therapies. As a result, humanistic counselling will need to demonstrate its effectiveness in order to compete with cognitive behavioural therapy (CBT) for viability and sustainability. Practitioners, however, remain hesitant to engage in research or to review findings; this is often referred to as 'the research to practice gap' in the literature.[13]

There is strong scientific support for counselling and psychotherapy as effective treatments for mental health issues. Counselling and psychotherapy research has largely focused on cognitive behavioural therapy and there is an emerging body of research that supports the utility of positive psychotherapy.[14] Both modalities have focused mainly on outcome research, evaluating the impact of the therapeutic approaches and interventions on symptom reduction and quality of life, respectively. We also know that different therapists achieve different outcomes with their clients, some consistently achieving better results than others.[15]

We return to the question – is it possible to heal emotional wounds through the use of a set of research-based techniques and strategies? The answer is, in general, yes. Psychotherapy is effective across all ages, from children to adults. We can confidently say that counselling and psychotherapy is effective, 8 out of 10 people who attend therapy will feel better. The not so good news is that there will be no change for 10% of clients and 10% of clients will feel worse after therapy.[16]

TEN TAKEAWAYS FROM TALK THERAPY RESEARCH

Bruce Wampold and Zac Imel[17] have summarised findings from research in counselling and psychotherapy in their book *The Great Psychotherapy Debate* published in 2015 (points 1–5).

1. Psychotherapy is extremely effective.
2. The effects of therapy are greater than the effects of some surgical and medical procedures.
3. Psychotherapy is as effective as medication for common mental health conditions, anxiety and depression.
4. There is evidence to support that psychodynamic approaches are effective for the treatment of depression and post-traumatic stress disorder and social anxiety.
5. Common factors of therapy such as the working alliance, empathic understanding and psychoeducation about a condition are strongly related to positive outcomes.
6. Mindfulness based cognitive therapy and long-term psychoanalytic therapy is beneficial for people with persistent depression.[18]
7. Online based CBT is effective for social anxiety.[19]
8. Outdoor nature-based interventions improve mental health outcomes.[20]
9. Online CBT is as effective as face-to-face CBT for depression.[21]
10. CBT is an effective treatment for depression in older adults.[22]

While the evidence is useful and welcome, there are still gaps in our knowledge in counselling and psychotherapy.

UNANSWERED QUESTIONS

Peter Fonagy from the University College London makes the point that establishing superiority of one method over another is a very difficult task.[23] Based on the available evidence, we can say that CBT and psychodynamic approaches have comparable outcomes, implying that they are similar in effectiveness. When reviewing meta-analysis (a review of several studies) on results of comparative psychotherapy outcome research, we need to be careful and take note of the differing populations and the type of studies conducted, in particular random clinical trials (RTCs), considered the gold standard when assessing outcome research. Research carried out by Bruce Wampold in 1997, following a review of 200 studies on different therapies, found the difference in terms of effectiveness on outcome was minimal, which led him to call this the Dodo Bird Verdict, meaning all (therapies) are winners, everyone wins prizes.[24] What this means is that all therapies have common factors, such as therapists are highly skilled, are empathic and therapists have the ability to create a close rapport with clients regardless of the approach. While we know that common factors in psychotherapy influence outcome, more research is needed to identify which factors have the greater influence on outcome and for whom. Research on digital therapy and artificial intelligence as a means of support is necessary to evaluate their utility, whether as stand-alone options or integrated into a blended model. In spite of the fact that psychological therapies are based on an extensive evidence base, research in this area is often complex and multifaceted, and sophisticated analyses of findings are required. There is considerable debate in the literature on the most appropriate methods for conducting research, as mentioned, while RCTs are considered the gold standard in outcome research, there is a call for more practice-based evidence. There are also discussions on the various aspects of psychodynamic therapy and how to approach it from a research perspective. Research is challenging and especially in the field of psychodynamic therapies, as there are many diverse types. This approach has been compared to real, if dysfunctional, families whose members have difficulties communicating with each other and sometimes speak different languages. How then can we compare and generalise findings from such a diverse group? It is important not only to understand what works, but also how it works (identification of mechanisms that allow change to occur) and for whom it works in order for the field to advance. It is imperative that we push the research agenda further in counselling and psychotherapy to investigate the relationship between individual differences and therapeutic processes and outcomes.

CONCLUSIONS

This chapter explained why we need research in counselling and psychotherapy, and it summarised what we have learned about talk therapy so far. As therapists, our choice of therapeutic approach should be informed by this information. Understanding how research works can help us critically evaluate findings and become more effective practitioners. Research in counselling and psychotherapy is vital, for sustainability and professionalism and to evaluate whether therapy is a worthwhile enterprise. While there is a large body of evidence which supports the effectiveness of therapy and we are better informed on the benefits of talk therapy for clients, there are questions that remain unanswered. More research is needed to consider who benefits most and what approach works best. Research is essential for the continued survival and development of counselling, as with any profession. It is through research that we can introduce new concepts in the field and challenge old ones and to find out what therapy works for which issue and for whom. As therapists we need to adopt a research mind-set. Helping practitioner professionals (psychologists, mental health practitioners, counsellors and psychotherapists) have a responsibility to add to the body of knowledge that exists in the field of therapy. Consumers of therapy can be assured that research-based therapies are available if and when needed. With so many scientific and therapeutic approaches available, it is necessary to be a critical consumer of these approaches.

What is promising is the vast amount of research in therapy that confirms not only its utility and effectiveness, but also the extraordinary ability of human beings to change, adapt and self-correct. This is in keeping with Rogers's ideas all those years ago, that human beings have an innate capacity to grow and actualise their potentialities, even if their efforts have been thwarted or pushed down.

NOTES

1 Paul (1967)
2 Mark (1996)
3 Gravetter and Forzano (2011)
4 Treger and Masciale (2018)
5 Gravetter and Forzano (2011, p. 7)
6 Gravetter and Forzano (2011)
7 Gravetter and Forzano (2011)
8 Mark (1996)
9 Gravetter and Forzano (2011)
10 Mark (1996)
11 Kirschenbaum (2007)
12 Cooper (2008)
13 Barker et al. (2010)
14 Seligman et al. (2005)
15 Wampold and Imel (2015)
16 Cooper (2008)
17 Wampold and Imel (2015)
18 McPherson and Senra (2022)
19 Nordgreen et al. (2018)
20 Coventry et al. (2021)
21 Luo et al. (2020)
22 Jayasekara et al. (2014)
23 Roth and Fonagy (2006)
24 Cooper (2008)

8

PROFESSIONAL ISSUES IN COUNSELLING AND PSYCHOTHERAPY

INTRODUCTION

So far, we have looked at several issues around counselling and psychotherapy and reviewed the four major approaches we use to help clients struggling with emotional or social problems. Those approaches have diverse ways of working based on human development and suffering assumptions. We have discussed the importance of a safe space with a compassionate, caring, qualified therapist to help clients talk about their personal and often painful history and thoughts. We spoke about how we, as therapists, work hard to provide unconditional positive regard and stay non-judgemental as clients reveal their life choices, thoughts, fears and behaviours. How do we do all of this and remain professional? What should we do if we are affected by what we hear in the therapy room? Let us try and answer these questions now.

COUNSELLOR – CLIENT DYNAMICS

Psychology, psychiatry, psychotherapy and counselling books and papers often tell us that there is a power differential in therapy in the client–counsellor relationship. Freud's theory of transference (see Chapter 2)

DOI: 10.4324/9781003196471-8

talks about how clients were encouraged to act out, or re-enact, their past relationships and project emotions onto the analyst. This reinforced the concept of a power differential and suggested a relationship between a strong therapist and a fragile, vulnerable client. This 'inherent power differential' is questionable, Ernest Jones, a prominent psychoanalyst, raised a concern about the assumption of therapists – he referred to this as the 'God syndrome' – where the therapist is the 'all knowing' or the 'wise knower.'[1] Many clients who come to us for help are depressed, anxious, traumatised or vulnerable. But some clients come to therapy to improve their relationships or quality of life and want help to find insight into their life choices. These people are not considered vulnerable; they are people who choose to use therapy for self-awareness and personal development. It is also worth remembering that power in any relationship is dynamic, constantly changing and not static. Professional therapists are responsible for providing their clients with the highest quality therapy, most ethically and safely possible and protecting them from harm, regardless of whether they are seen as vulnerable. We, therapists, do this for ourselves in a number of ways outside of our therapy space by engaging in continuing professional development after we qualify, attending regular clinical supervision and becoming members of professional bodies. Within the therapy space, we work to our professional best. We ensure that each client understands the 'contract' at the first session. We clarify, establish and maintain physical, emotional and social boundaries.

PHYSICAL AND SOCIAL BOUNDARIES

The concept of a professional relationship with boundaries between a therapist and a client is a key part of counselling training and practice. In Chapter 1, we discussed contracting at the first counselling session, where the key issues around attendance, frequency and duration of therapy are agreed upon. Contracting with a client at the first session also provides an opportunity to discuss the client's expectations of therapy and the importance of boundaries. This can help avoid any awkwardness or unpleasantness with a potential boundary violation.

All of us in our professional life and work need to establish and maintain safe relationships with others and be mindful of the limitations of these relationships. Therapists do not enter into personal friendships or sexual relationships with clients. We should not work with someone if we know them or work with them in another role – for example, we will not provide therapy for a work colleague or a friend. In the therapy setting, we need to be friendly without being friends. We do not rescue or try to 'fix' clients. We do not collude with clients or behave in a way that extends the therapeutic relationship or work for longer than necessary.[2] Regardless of our therapeutic orientation and working methods, we make sure that we are caring. Still, we also retain the ability to challenge deeply held assumptions or beliefs or patterns of relating to others if, when and where appropriate.

Unlike Tess and Eliza, the robots from Chapter 6, the therapist is a human being with their own history and experiences of sadness and emotional pain. We can also become affected by our clients' experiences, which is especially true when we work with people who have experienced particularly traumatic events and situations in their lives. We are never sure what our clients may bring to a session. They may tell us they have one issue at the beginning of therapy and then speak about another devastating experience weeks or months later. As therapists, we need to be prepared and grounded to have measured responses to our clients' stories and not express shock or dismay at disclosures. We need to be careful when a client's experience triggers an emotional response and know how to manage that appropriately. Having a clear understanding of what belongs to the client and the therapist's issue is crucial in working effectively and safely. It is essential that therapists can feel and can show genuine empathy and understanding of the client's experiences and, at the same time, avoid becoming caught up in their emotional world. To do this, we need to be mindful of our own personal and emotional lives, practice self-care to prevent burnout and talk with our clinical supervisors about the impact of our work. Professional therapists must ensure they have boundaries in place and seek counselling for themselves if they are experiencing emotional upheaval in their personal lives.[3]

ACCOUNTABILITY

Transparency and accountability in counselling and psychotherapy are essential for those working as professional helpers. We must maintain accurate and appropriate records, which shows our commitment to the client and our respect for their information. It also offers an appreciation of the uniqueness and value of each client by protecting their confidentiality and privacy. We must explain to our clients how their data will be stored and how their privacy will be protected. This helps to build their trust in the therapist and the therapy. Confidentiality is paramount, and clients have a right to expect their details and the information they have shared with a therapist to be safe. However, there are times when it may be appropriate to break confidentiality, for example, when there is a risk of harm to the client or others. We must make sure our clients understand this from the first consultation. They should also be informed of what to expect from the therapeutic process and other issues such as costs, duration, frequency and expected therapeutic benefits.

ETHICAL ISSUES

There are a number of professional bodies in Counselling and Psychotherapy. The largest in the United Kingdom is the British Association of Counselling and Psychotherapy (BACP) or United Kingdom Counselling and Psychotherapy (UKCP) and the Irish Association of Counselling and Psychotherapy (IACP) or the Irish Council for Psychotherapy (ICP) in Ireland. Registered members of professional accrediting bodies use their professional, ethical frameworks for good practice. When you become a member of a professional organisation, you tell the world that you believe in, and work within, the organisation's professional values, principles and code of conduct.

Earlier in this book, we looked at the importance of the therapeutic relationship, or the therapeutic alliance, as it is often referred to in the literature.[4] Therapy is not just about creating a warm atmosphere or a friendly environment to help the client talk about personal issues in their life. There needs to be a level of trust between clients and therapists about sensitive information about their well-being. Psychotherapists must work in the best interests of their clients and use the best and most appropriate methods to help them achieve their goals. Trustworthiness is a serious ethical commitment, and members of professional bodies agree to abide by the code of conduct, behave ethically and avoid causing harm to clients. Therapists agree that their clients' needs are their primary concern, to provide the best possible service and uphold professional standards. This means that we work within our competencies and take measures to continue our own professional development by keeping our skills and knowledge up to date.

Working within boundaries can be challenging for both clients and therapists. Counselling and psychotherapy provide a safe, confidential space where the relationship between the therapist and the client is important, even if the relationship is different for each client. Take social relationships: If you disclose personal information to someone, you create an emotional bond. But if a therapist discloses their own personal information to one of their clients, it can shift the focus of attention and might be violating boundaries. In Chapter 2, Freud sees the analyst as a neutral figure, a blank slate to encourage a transfer of emotional content from the clients' past significant relationships to address inner conflict and tension associated with that relationship. In classic psychoanalysis, the therapist does not share information about themselves at any point. By contrast, Rogers believed that person-centred therapy needed to be a two-way process. The therapists should disclose any feelings that might arise during the therapy if it is in the client's best interest. The 'use of self' is a term often used by humanistic and relational therapists. It means that the therapist draws on their own experiences and personality to enhance the therapeutic process for the client. So, in this way, therapists can share some of their own experiences, but only if it is in the client's best interest and will help the client move towards awareness or insight, and not because it meets the needs of the therapists.

ETHICAL ISSUES TO CONSIDER WITH A NEW CLIENT

When meeting a client for the first time, a therapist should reflect on some questions. These questions can form part of the initial assessment and give a sense of the 'goodness of fit' between the client and counsellor. Halgin and Caron (1991)[5] suggest the following:

1. Does this person need therapy?
2. Do I know the person? Or do they know someone in my close social network?
3. What is my personal reaction to the person?
4. Am I emotionally capable and available for this person?
5. Does the person feel comfortable with me?

During this process, the therapist explores ethical issues and their capacity to work with the person's particular problem and their actual ability to do so.

THE THERAPEUTIC RELATIONSHIP – WHEN THINGS GO WRONG

Counselling can be challenging for both the client and the therapist. Sometimes there is tension in the client–counsellor relationship, especially when you are working together for a number of weeks or months. There can be gradual changes in behaviour, feelings and perspective. Sometimes clients may feel frustrated or impatient if there is little or no progress after a few consultations. Often, they will experience intense emotions as they recall events or problems in their lives and react negatively towards the therapist. There may be a time when a therapist overlooked something or was inadvertently unaware of an issue that was important to the client, leaving them feeling their experience was not understood or considered important. Therapists may feel they are not the right person for a particular client, or they may interpret the client's negative emotions as a personal attack.

Conflict and tension in the client–counsellor relationship are sometimes called a 'rupture' or a break in a previously harmonious relationship. While a breakdown in the relationship can vary in terms of quality and intensity, a rupture in the relationship, although unpleasant, can be an opportunity to work through the difficulty and for both parties to learn and grow. Research by Jeremy Safran and colleagues (2011) found that ruptures are common in all types of therapy. If a client loses trust in the therapist, the client may drop out of therapy abruptly.[6] However, clients are reluctant to raise any negative issues, and therapists sometimes fail to notice early warning signs of a client's dissatisfaction. The therapist's engagement in self-reflection ensures that they can critically evaluate their practice and their own process when working with clients, which could potentially increase their awareness of problems or growing tensions in their relationship with a client.

REFLECTIVE PRACTICE

Therapists regularly practice self-reflection; it's integral to the profession of therapy. We reflect on our clients, and we think about how our clients became the people they are, and we also reflect about our own lives and how we became the person we are.[7] Reflective practice is something that happens in most professions, and, in counselling and psychotherapy, it encourages us to reflect on our professional and personal experiences as therapists and evaluate the quality of our work with clients. To maintain and uphold the values and standards of our profession, the reflective practice supports our ongoing professional development, examines behaviours and attitudes as therapists, as well as those of the client and identifies where we can change or improve. Separating what belongs to the client from the therapist's unresolved issue is essential in therapy. Reflective practice gives us a developmental opportunity – not every approach will work with every client – it helps us recognise tension or even a breakdown in the relationship with a client, resolve it and prevent it from happening again. Reflective practice allows us to consider what has worked well with clients and what needs to be changed.

The opportunity for therapists to reflect on their work with clients is not limited to self-reflection, as regular supervision is a requirement for professional therapists. This entails regular meetings with experienced and qualified supervisors to reflect on their practice critically. Although a formal structured arrangement, supervision is generally supportive and helps promote the therapist's professional development and ensure professional standards are upheld for the safety and welfare of clients.

SAFE PRACTICE

A theme throughout this book has been the importance of the therapeutic relationship and the ability of a therapist to be empathic and understand someone else's suffering. As mentioned in Chapter 1, being a professional therapist can be extremely rewarding and incredibly challenging. Although compassion is not confined to therapists, it is key to our professional work. It is not surprising that people drawn to working as professional therapists are usually compassionate people by nature and care about people and want to help others in their time of need, although there can be a personal cost when giving becomes too much.

THE COST OF CARING

'Compassion fatigue' is characterised by physical and emotional exhaustion and a significant reduction in empathy for clients, co-workers and loved ones. It is accompanied by a decline in professional satisfaction and eventually may develop into depression, secondary traumatic stress and stress-related illnesses.[8] Symptoms of compassion fatigue can be harmful because they target our primary motivation for participating in this work: empathy. Compassion fatigue is referred to as the 'cost of caring' by Figley.[9] It is an occupational hazard, and almost every person providing care will experience it to varying degrees. But compassion fatigue is not confined to professional therapists. Other people in helping professions (such as firefighters, members of the police force, nurses, social workers and many others) can experience it too. The best way to prevent or mitigate it is to use self-care strategies, without which we are at risk of compassion fatigue and burnout, and you need to keep a wary eye out for the warning signs. Although symptoms vary depending on the person, they include a reduced ability to feel sympathy and empathy, anger and irritability at loved ones, increased use of alcohol and drugs, dread of working with specific clients and diminished work satisfaction.[10]

The development of compassion fatigue and recovery from it are gradual processes. While some people can be restored by taking a break or taking some time off work, most people must make lifestyle changes, establish and maintain boundaries with co-workers and others and prioritise their own health and wellness.[11]

GOOD PRACTICE AND BEST PRACTICE

We have already talked about how therapists practice therapy and how they strive to maintain a professional attitude. Part of being a professional is to reflect on our practice regularly and distinguish between 'good practice' (working safely) and 'best practice' (the best way to work with clients). Naturally, we want to treat clients with respect and empathy, acknowledge diversity and ensure that we work in a way that does not cause harm.

As counselling and psychotherapy developed, many schools vied for attention, all with their own unique language that was only understood by those who supported their views. A separatist adversarial culture prevailed, and dogmas were proclaimed.[12] The competition between certain schools in counselling and psychotherapy remains today. Naturally, no one school or orientation has all the answers to all the problems for all the people.

Regardless of the depth of experience and highly developed skills of a therapist in a particular modality, no single orientation has been able to demonstrate universal success.[13] The entire field remains fragmented and divisive, not only in defining counselling as different to psychotherapy but also in terms of 'the right way' to help people or the 'best' form of therapy. Recently two position papers were drafted by two of the leading professional bodies in Ireland.[14] One asserts that psychotherapy and counselling are distinct professions, with various competencies and expertise,[15] and the other maintains there is no difference between counselling and psychotherapy.[16] The only way to resolve this conflicting view is through dialogue and debate. In reality, therapists need to be competent in and comfortable with various methods to meet the challenges they face in their profession.[17] There are currently more than 400 approaches to counselling and psychotherapy. And as the field evolves, new therapies and ideas emerge about what works and who benefits from them. Prochaska and Norcross (2018) summarise it nicely:

> Students, practitioners, and clients face confusion, fragmentation, and discontent. With so many therapies and approaches claiming success, which theories should be studied, taught, or bought?[18]

In previous chapters, we have seen various ideas and methods from different models of therapy that can facilitate healing and change. You will find research to support most of these approaches (see Chapter 7), and they all have value and offer insight into human development and suffering. But so many approaches can be a problem for some therapists who believe there is 'no one size to fit us all.' They cannot even agree on which is the most effective, even though there is often a minor difference in terms of effectiveness between the primary schools of counselling. Some therapists refer to themselves as 'eclectic' because they use more than one theoretical approach or technique to help their clients. Others work in an 'integrative' way, combining different elements of therapeutic approaches in their work with each client. McLeod (2013)[19] asks, should a counsellor focus on only one approach to become as effective as possible in one model of therapy? If the answer is yes, what about the other methods and techniques from different approaches that have been effective? Even though eclectic and integrative therapy approaches do not focus on single orientation approaches, they are still concerned about what they think might be helpful and not about what the client may think or how they may like to work. Therapists interested in a pluralistic approach must be open and flexible to what each client needs, as opposed to rigidly sticking to one approach every time.[20]

A PLURALISTIC APPROACH TO COUNSELLING

The following discussion is informed by Mick Cooper and John McLeod's work on their pluralistic approach to counselling,[21,22] both leading figures in the field. Choosing a pluralistic approach implies putting clients at the centre of power and choice in practical terms. Pluralism is not about 'let us try something else,' it's an attitude to how we see our clients and their involvement in the therapeutic planning and process. Complex issues might need two or more therapeutic approaches to resolve. The pluralistic approach starts from the assumption that different things are likely to help other people at different points.

In contrast, a single perspective on the client's problems allows little or no space for other well-established methods to be used. Pluralism in counselling emphasises the importance of an open dialogue between the therapist and the client about how to best approach problems from the client's standpoint. It is common for counsellors to explore their goals for counselling with clients and how these relate to the client's life in general. Therapists usually spend a great deal of time building trust and rapport with the client and understanding their desired goals.

A pluralistic position looks at as many options as possible to help clients. A pluralistic approach implies several ways to approach a client's issue, and there is a lot of research to support this assertion. A client usually consults a therapist when their efforts to solve a problem have been unsuccessful or not as effective as they would have liked. From a therapist's perspective, it is important to remember the uniqueness of each client, their individual needs and histories and their repertoire of coping skills that have worked well in the past. Other problems and other available strategies go beyond the counsellor's first ideas, many of which would not usually occur in the therapy room. For example, as we have looked at in Chapter 6, walking outdoors or visiting green or blue spaces might be useful to consider.

When a practitioner takes a pluralistic approach, they examine the client's perspective on their problem and what sort of change strategies would be most or least helpful. They also explore the resources the client has and is most comfortable with and where their limitations might be. This gives a shared understanding of the issue and a mutually agreed way of working, with appropriate strategies and interventions unique to the individual's circumstances and needs. McLeod (2013)[23] outlines a set of issues the pluralistic counsellor needs to address in their conversations with clients:

- Develop a shared understanding of the problem in living that has led the person to seek therapy.
- Explore the goals of the client – in what direction are they moving in their life? What do they want to get from therapy? What are their purposes and intentions in relation to therapy?
- How can these goals be broken down into step-by-step tasks, the completion of which will contribute to the achievement of each goal?
- What are the methods through which tasks can be fulfilled? What activities can the therapist and the client engage in to enable task completion?

We are seeing increased research on clients' perceptions of therapy and, more recently, on their preferences because we recognise and try to facilitate the client's autonomy, respecting their wish to be active participants in the therapeutic process. The client's therapy preferences are also considered with a pluralistic approach. They are guided by their beliefs and attitudes to make choices and decisions about their willingness and limitations to engage in their therapy and any interventions.

The research suggests that client preferences influence counselling outcomes in two ways. One, when a client's preferred methods of working are used, there are lower dropout rates, and abrupt premature endings are less likely. Two, according to Cooper and Norcross (2021), clients are more likely to successfully manage their problems when offered a choice in methods and their preferred approach or method is considered. It is important to note that there are several reasons why clients end therapy. They may feel therapy is not beneficial, they may think that they have too many things to do between sessions (especially with CBT) and they do not want to report on progress at every session. They may feel a sense of pressure to confirm the model. Some clients may not like the lack of interventions in person-centred counselling. They may feel a lack of practical strategies to try out on their own time and a lack of direction or the absence of problem-solving skills doesn't suit their needs or personality. We humans are complex and different and some of us see strengths in one therapy that others view as weaknesses.

A single approach to therapy, according to Cooper and Dryden (2016) is limited in terms of what it can offer a client. Today, clients can be far more knowledgeable about the range of healing and change options available. What was relevant half a decade ago may not have the same relevance now. Being truly person-centred in contemporary counselling does not mean you have to stick rigidly to Rogers's approach. Instead, person-centred means actively involving the client in their therapeutic process – not the same as CBT therapists would do, which is an agreed agenda and a collaborative process with clients. While the client in CBT is an active participant in the work and there is an agreed agenda on the methods, it is conducted against the backdrop of the CBT model and to the exclusion of other approaches or strategies that a client may find helpful. Most counselling approaches have much to offer in terms of change and healing and adopting one should not mean excluding another method.

CONCLUSIONS

In this chapter, we have seen that counselling and psychotherapy is a professional undertaking. Every effort is made by professional accrediting bodies to ensure the safety and welfare of clients and the learning and development of therapists. Professional counsellors join the professional body, adhere to its ethical framework and guidelines, and attend supervision regularly. In the 1950s, Carl Rogers popularised the term 'unconditional positive regard.' Since then, it has become a part of the culture of counselling and can be viewed as inherent to the ethics of our profession. However, as in all relationships, conflict can arise between the client and the counsellor. Working through conflict and tension or problems that occur in the client–counsellor relationship, although uncomfortable, can be immensely helpful in developing greater self-awareness and insight for both the client and the therapist. We also looked at the importance of being open to considering well-established techniques and interventions from other therapeutic approaches. We discussed how therapists appreciate diversity concerning clients, culture, and social context, yet single oriented approaches can be fixed in ideas and views about what might be helpful to clients. If we, as therapists, are to be genuinely open to learning and tolerant of others, this must extend to the theories and practice of therapy. The concept of pluralism has implications for the theory and practice of counselling, training and research.

FINAL THOUGHTS

The importance of good mental health and psychological well-being cannot be overstated. Knowing that there is support available when life is not going well is important; knowing the different types of available support when seeking professional help is essential. Further reading and web resources page is a good place to start if you would like to find out about some of the issues presented here. I hope that you found this book useful in some way and that it has given you a better understanding of counselling, but there is more information to share – you can access my blog for up-to-date news and views on topics covered in this book at www.mppsychologicalservices.com

Let's continue our conversation about counselling.

NOTES

1 Jones (1960)
2 Kennedy and Charles (2002)
3 Kennedy and Charles (2002)
4 McLeod (2013)
5 Halgin and Caron (1991)
6 Safran et al. (2011)
7 Claringbull (2010)
8 Sinclair et al. (2017)
9 Figley (2015)
10 Sinclair et al. (2017)
11 Sinclair et al. (2017)
12 Finnerty et al. (2018)
13 Wampold and Imel (2015)
14 Finnerty et al. (2018 p 13)
15 Irish Association of Counselling and Psychotherapy (IACP 2015)
16 The Irish Council for Psychotherapy (ICP 2015)
17 Finnerty et al. (2018)
18 Prochaska and Norcross (2018, p. 1)
19 McLeod (2013)
20 Cooper and Dryden (2016)
21 Cooper and McLeod (2007)
22 McLeod (2017)
23 McLeod (2013, p. 293)

FURTHER READING AND WEB RESOURCES

The following are useful resources on topics presented in each chapter.

CHAPTER 1 COUNSELLING – PAST, PRESENT AND FUTURE

Books

McLeod, J. (2019). *Introduction to counselling*. Open University Press.

Websites

British Association of Counselling and Psychotherapy (BACP) www.bacp.co.uk
Irish Association of Counselling and Psychotherapy (IACP) www.iacp.ie
American Psychological Association – History of Psychology www.apa.org
Diagnostic Statistical Manual of Mental Health Disorders www.psychiatry.org

CHAPTER 2 FREUD REVIEWED AND RECONSIDERED

Books

Gay, P. (1989). *Freud: A life of our times*. Papermac.
Mitchell, A., & Black, M. (2016). *Freud and beyond*. Basic Books.

Websites

International Psychoanalysis Association (IPA) – www.ipa.world
Neuropsychoanalysis Society Association (NPSA) – www.npsa-association.org
Association of Psychoanalysis and Psychotherapy in Ireland – www.appi.ie

CHAPTER 3 HUMANISTIC PSYCHOLOGY – A PERSON-CENTRED APPROACH

Books

Cooper, M., O'Hara, M., Schmid, P., & Bohart, A. (2013). *Handbook of person-centred counselling* (2nd ed.). Bloomsbury Academic.
Maslow, A. (2011). *Toward a psychology of being*. Martino Publishing.

Websites

Carl Rogers – www.carlrrogers.org
Carl Rogers and Natalie Rogers – www.carlrogersphd.com
World Association for Person Centered and Experiential Psychotherapy and Counselling
www.pce-world.org
The International Focusing Institute – building on the work of Eugene Gendlin since 1979
https://focusing.org/more/about-institute

CHAPTER 4 COGNITIVE BEHAVIOURAL THERAPY

Books

Beck, J. S., & Beck, A. (2020). *Cognitive behavioural therapy: Basics and beyond*. Guildford Press.
Greenberger, D., & Padesky, C. (2015). *Mind over mood*. Guildford Press.
Hayes, S. (2012). *Get out of your mind and into your life*. Read How You Want.

Websites

Beck Institute – https://beckinstitute.org
Albert Ellis institute – https://albertellis.org
Steven Hayes – https://stevenchayes.com
Association for Contextual Behavioural Science https://contextualscience.org/
    steve_hayes
Marsha Linehan DBT
www.psychwire.com/linehan
Christine Padesky – www.padesky.com

CHAPTER 5 THE PROMISE OF POSITIVE PSYCHOLOGY

Books

Seligman, M. (2011). *Flourish, a new understanding of happiness and well-being – and how to achieve them: A new understanding of happiness and wellbeing: The practical . . . psychology to make you happier and healthier.* Nicholas Brealey Publishing.
Rashid, T., & Seligman, M. (2018). *Positive psychology manual.* Oxford University Press.
Harris, R. (2022). *The happiness trap.* Robinson Publishing.

Websites

Positive Psychology Center – University of Pennsylvania – www.ppc.sas.
    upenn.edu
Pursuit of Happiness – Martin Seligman – www.pursuit-of-happiness.org

CHAPTER 6 THE HEALING SPACE – A CHANGING LANDSCAPE

Books

Jordan, M. (2016). *Ecotherapy: Theory research and practice.* Palgrave.
Clinebell, H. (2013). *Healing ourselves, healing the earth.* Routledge.
McGeeney, A. (2016). *With nature in mind: The ecotherapy manual for mental health professionals.* Jessica Kingsley Publishers.

Websites

Nature Therapy Online – www.naturetherapyonline.net/scotlandherapy

Nature Based Therapy, Reconnect Learn and Grow – www.naturebasedtherapy.com.au

CHAPTER 7 RESEARCH IN COUNSELLING AND PSYCHOTHERAPY

Books

McLeod, J. (2022). *Doing research in counselling and psychotherapy*. Sage.

Websites

British Association of Counselling and Psychotherapy – www.bacp.co.uk

CHAPTER 8 PROFESSIONAL ISSUES

Books

Cooper, M., & Dryden, W. (2015). *The handbook of pluralistic counselling and psychotherapy*. SAGE.

Norcross, J., & VandenBos, G. (2018). *Leaving it at the office, a guide to psychotherapist self-care*. Guildford Press.

McLeod, J., & McLeod, J. (2014). *Personal and professional development for counsellors, psychotherapists, and mental health practitioners*. Open University Press.

Finlay, L. (2021). *The therapeutic use of self*. Sage.

Websites

Pluralistic Counselling – www.pluralisticpractice.com

British Association of Counselling and Psychotherapy – www.bacp.com

Irish Association of Counselling and Psychotherapy – www.iacp.ie

REFERENCES

American Psychiatric Association. (2013). *Diagnostic and statistical manual of mental disorders, fifth edition (DSM-5(TM))* (5th ed.). American Psychiatric Publishing.

Banks, J. (2018). The human touch: Practical and ethical implications of putting AI and robotics to work for patients. *IEEE Pulse, 9*(3), 15–18. https://doi.org/10.1109/mpul.2018.2814238

Barker, G. G., & Barker, E. E. (2021). Online therapy: Lessons learned from the COVID-19 health crisis. *British Journal of Guidance & Counselling, 50*(1), 66–81. https://doi.org/10.1080/03069885.2021.1889462

Barker, M., Vossler, A., Langdridge, D., & Barker, M. (2010). *Understanding counselling and psychotherapy (published in association with the open university)* (1st ed.). SAGE Publications Ltd.

Baumeister, R. F., Bratslavsky, E., Finkenauer, C., & Vohs, K. D. (2001). Bad is stronger than good. *Review of General Psychology, 5*(4), 323–370. https://doi.org/10.1037/1089-2680.5.4.323

Beck, A. T., Rush, J. A., Shaw, B. F., & Emery, G. (1987). *Cognitive therapy of depression (the Guilford clinical psychology and psychopathology series)* (1st ed.). The Guilford Press.

Beck, J. S., & Beck, A. T. (2020). *Cognitive behavior therapy: Basics and beyond* (3rd ed.). The Guilford Press.

Bethell, C., Jones, J., Gombojav, N., Linkenbach, J., & Sege, R. (2019). Positive childhood experiences and adult mental and relational health in a statewide sample. *JAMA Pediatrics*, 173(11), e193007. https://doi.org/10.1001/jamapediatrics.2019.3007

British Association for Counselling and Psychotherapy. (2013). BACP. Definition of Counselling. Lutterworth, Retrieved January 4, 2022, from available at http://www.bacp.co.uk.

Carver, C. S., Scheier, M. F., & Segerstrom, S. C. (2010). Optimism. *Clinical Psychology Review*, 30(7), 879–889. https://doi.org/10.1016/j.cpr.2010.01.006

Chaudhury, P., & Banerjee, D. (2020). "Recovering with nature": A review of ecotherapy and implications for the COVID-19 pandemic. *Frontiers in Public Health*, 8. https://doi.org/10.3389/fpubh.2020.604440

Claringbull, N. (2010). *What is counselling and psychotherapy? (Counselling and psychotherapy practice series)* (1st ed.). Learning Matters.

Clements-Hickman, A. L., & Reese, R. J. (2022). The person of the therapist: Therapists' personal characteristics as predictors of alliance and treatment outcomes. *Psychotherapy Research*, 1–12. https://doi.org/10.1080/10503307.2022.2080610

Clinebell, H. (1996). *Ecotherapy: Healing ourselves, healing the earth* (1st ed.). Routledge.

Cooper, M. (2008). *Essential research findings in counselling and psychotherapy: The facts are friendly*. Sage Pubns (in association with BACP).

Cooper, M., & Dryden, W. (2016). *The handbook of pluralistic counselling and psychotherapy* (1st ed.). SAGE Publications Ltd.

Cooper, M., & McLeod, J. (2007). A pluralistic framework for counselling and psychotherapy: Implications for research. *Counselling and Psychotherapy Research*, 7(3), 135–143. https://doi.org/10.1080/14733140701566282

Coventry, P. A., Brown, J., Pervin, J., Brabyn, S., Pateman, R., Breedvelt, J., . . . White, P. (2021). Nature-based outdoor activities for mental and physical health: Systematic review and meta-analysis. *SSM – Population Health*, 16, 100934. https://doi.org/10.1016/j.ssmph.2021.100934

Crocq, M. A., & Crocq, L. (2000). From shell shock and war neurosis to post-traumatic stress disorder: A history of psychotraumatology. *Dialogues in Clinical Neuroscience*, 2(1), 47–55. https://doi.org/10.31887/dcns.2000.2.1/macrocq

Csikszentmihalyi, M. (2008). *Flow: The psychology of optimal experience (harper perennial modern classics)* (1st ed.). Harper Perennial Modern Classics.

Ellis, A., & Ellis, D. J. (2011). *Rational emotive behavior therapy (theories of psychotherapy)* (1st ed.). Amer Psychological Assn.

Felitti, V. J., Anda, R. F., Nordenberg, D., Williamson, D. F., Spitz, A. M., . . . Marks, J. S. (1998). Relationship of childhood abuse and household dysfunction to many of the leading causes of death in adults. *American Journal of Preventive Medicine*, 14(4), 245–258. https://doi.org/10.1016/s0749-3797(98)00017-8

Figley, C. R. (2015). *Treating compassion fatigue (Brunner-Routledge psychosocial stress)* (1st ed.). Routledge.

Finnerty, M., Kearns, C., & O'Regan, D. (2018). *Pluralism: An ethical commitment to dialogue and collaboration*. IACP. Retrieved January 3, 2022, from Pluralism-An-ethical-commitment-to-dialogue-and-collaboration-by-Dr.M.Finnerty-Caitriona-Kearns-and-David-ORegan.pdf(iacp.ie)

Fischer, B. A. (2012). A review of American psychiatry through its diagnoses. *Journal of Nervous & Mental Disease*, 200(12), 1022–1030. https://doi.org/10.1097/nmd.0b013e318275cf19

Gay, P. (1998). *Freud: A life for our time*. W. W. Norton & Company.

Gravetter, F. J., & Forzano, L. B. (2011). *Research methods for the behavioural sciences* (4th ed.). Cengage Learning.

Greenberger, D., Padesky, C. A., & Beck, A. T. (2015). *Mind over mood, second edition: Change how you feel by changing the way you think* (2nd ed.). The Guilford Press.

Halgin, R. P., & Caron, M. (1991). To treat or not to treat: Considerations for referring prospective clients. *Psychotherapy in Private Practice*, 8(4), 87–96.

Hanley, T. (2020). Researching online counselling and psychotherapy: The past, the present and the future. *Counselling and Psychotherapy Research*, 21(3), 493–497. https://doi.org/10.1002/capr.12385

Hayes, S. C., & Smith, S. (2005). *Get out of your mind and into your life: The new acceptance and commitment therapy (a new harbinger self-help workbook)* (1st ed.). New Harbinger Publications.

Hayes, S. C., Strosahl, K. D., & Wilson, K. G. (2016). *Acceptance and commitment therapy, second edition: The process and practice of mindful change* (2nd ed.). The Guilford Press.

Hazlegreaves, S. (2020). *The future of therapy: Online counselling searches increase by 124%*. Open Access Government. Retrieved February 2, 2022, from www.openaccessgovernment.org/the-future-of-therapy-online-counselling.

Hergenhahn, B. R. (1994). *An introduction to theories of personality* (4th ed.). Prentice Hall.

IACP. (2015). *Irish association for counselling and psychotherapy: Position paper on statutory regulation*. www. irish-counselling.ie. IACP-PositionPaper-on-Regulation-and-the-Difference-betweenCounselling-and-Psychotherapy-January -2022.

ICP. (2015). *Irish council for psychotherapy: Position paper on statutory regulation and the distinction between the related professions of counselling and psychotherapy.* www.irish-counselling.ie/files/UserFiles/IACPPosition-Paper-on-Regulation-and-the-Difference between-Counselling-and-Psychotherapy-January -2022

Jayasekara, R., Procter, N., Harrison, J., Skelton, K., Hampel, S., Draper, R., & Deuter, K. (2014). Cognitive behavioural therapy for older adults with depression: A review. *Journal of Mental Health*, 24(3), 168–171. https://doi.org/10.3109/09638237.2014.971143

Jones, E. (1960). *The life and work of Sigmund Freud (three volume set).* Basic Books.

Joseph, S. (2015). *Positive therapy: Building bridges between positive psychology and person-centred psychotherapy* (2nd ed.). Routledge.

Kamitsis, I., & Simmonds, J. G. (2017). Using resources of nature in the counselling room: Qualitative research into ecotherapy practice. *International Journal for the Advancement of Counselling*, 39(3), 229–248. https://doi.org/10.1007/s10447-017-9294-y

Kennedy, E., & Charles, S. C. (2002). *On becoming a counsellor: A basic guide for non-professional counsellors and the helping professions* (3rd ed.). Gill & MacMillan.

Kennerley, H., Kirk, J., & Westbrook, D. (2017). *An introduction to cognitive behaviour therapy: Skills and applications* (3rd ed.). SAGE Publications Ltd.

Kirschenbaum, H. (2007). *The life and work of Carl Rogers by Howard Kirschenbaum.* Pccs Books.

Lilienfeld, S. O., Lynn, S. J., Ruscio, J., & Beyerstein, B. L. (2009). *50 Great myths of popular psychology: Shattering widespread misconceptions about human behavior* (1st ed.). Wiley-Blackwell.

Lillard, A. S., & Erisir, A. (2011). Old dogs learning new tricks: Neuroplasticity beyond the juvenile period. *Developmental Review*, 31(4), 207–239. https://doi.org/10.1016/j.dr.2011.07.008

Lmft, B. S. (2022). *DBT explained: An introduction to essential dialectical behavior therapy concepts, practices, and skills.* Rockridge Press.

Luo, C., Sanger, N., Singhal, N., Pattrick, K., Shams, I., Shahid, H., . . . Samaan, Z. (2020). A comparison of electronically-delivered and face to face cognitive behavioural therapies in depressive disorders: A systematic review and meta-analysis. *EClinicalMedicine*, 24, 100442. https://doi.org/10.1016/j.eclinm.2020.100442

Mark, R. (1996). *Research made simple: A handbook for social workers* (1st ed.). SAGE Publications, Inc.

Maslow, A. (1943). A theory of human motivation. *Psychological Review*, 50, 370–396.

McGeeney, A. (2016). *With nature in mind: The ecotherapy manual for mental health professionals*. Jessica Kingsley Publishers.

McLeod, J. (2013). *An introduction to counselling* (5th ed., rev., updated). Open University Press.

McLeod, J. (2017). *Pluralistic therapy: Distinctive features*. Routledge.

McPherson, S., & Senra, H. (2022). Psychological treatments for persistent depression: A systematic review and meta-analysis of quality of life and functioning outcomes. *Psychotherapy*, 59(3), 447–459. https://doi.org/10.1037/pst0000448

Mearns, D., & Cooper, M. (2017). *Working at relational depth in counselling and psychotherapy* (2nd ed.). SAGE Publications Ltd.

Meichenbaum, D. (1977). Cognitive behaviour modification. *Scandinavian Journal of Behaviour Therapy*, 6(4), 185–192. https://doi.org/10.1080/16506073.1977.9626708

Merry, T. (2020). *Learning and being in person-centred counselling* (3rd ed.). PCCS Books.

Moncrieff, J., Cooper, R. E., Stockmann, T., Amendola, S., Hengartner, M. P., & Horowitz, M. A. (2022). The serotonin theory of depression: A systematic umbrella review of the evidence. *Molecular Psychiatry*. https://doi.org/10.1038/s41380-022-01661-0

Monte, C. F., & Sollod, R. N. (2003). *Beneath the mask: An introduction to theories of personality* (7th ed.). Wiley.

Nagarajan, M., & Yuvaraj, S. (2021). Mental health counsellors' perceptions on use of technology in counselling. *Current Psychology*, 40(4), 1760–1766. https://doi.org/10.1007/s12144-018-0104-4

Norcross, J. C., & Cooper, M. (2021). *Personalizing psychotherapy: Assessing and accommodating patient preferences*. American Psychological Association.

Nordgreen, T., Gjestad, R., Andersson, G., Carlbring, P., & Havik, O. E. (2018). The effectiveness of guided internet-based cognitive behavioral therapy for social anxiety disorder in a routine care setting. *Internet Interventions*, 13, 24–29. https://doi.org/10.1016/j.invent.2018.05.003

Paul, G. L. (1967). Strategy of outcome research in psychotherapy. *Journal of Consulting Psychology*, 31(2), 109–118. https://doi.org/10.1037/h0024436

Peseschkian, N. (1987). *Positive psychotherapy: Theory and practice of a new method*. Springer Verlag.

Peterson, C., & Seligman, M. (2004). *Character strengths and virtues: A handbook and classification* (1st ed.). American Psychological Association/Oxford University Press.

Prochaska, J. O., & Norcross, J. C. (2018). *Systems of psychotherapy: A transtheoretical analysis* (9th ed.). Oxford University Press.

Rashid, T., & Seligman, P. M. (2018). *Positive psychotherapy: Clinician manual.* Oxford University Press.

Rayce, S. B., Rasmussen, I. S., Klest, S. K., Patras, J., & Pontoppidan, M. (2017). Effects of parenting interventions for at-risk parents with infants: A systematic review and meta-analyses. *BMJ Open, 7*(12), e015707. https://doi.org/10.1136/bmjopen-2016-015707

Rogers, C. R. (1961). *On becoming a person: A therapist's view of psychotherapy.* Houghton Mifflin.

Rogers, C. R. (1963a). The actualizing tendency in relation to "motives" and to consciousness. In M. Jones (Ed.), *Nebraska symposium on motivation* (pp. 1–24, Vol. 11). U. Nebraska Press

Rogers, C. R. (1963b). The concept of the fully functioning person. *Psychotherapy: Theory, Research & Practice, 1*(1), 17–26. https://doi.org/10.1037/h0088567

Roth, A., & Fonagy, P. (2006). *What works for whom? A critical review of psychotherapy research.* Guilford Publications.

Safran, J. D., Muran, J. C., & Eubanks-Carter, C. (2011). Repairing alliance ruptures. *Psychotherapy, 48*(1), 80–87. https://doi.org/10.1037/a0022140

Sanders, P. (2022). *Tribes of the person-centred nation* (2nd rev. ed.). PCCS Books.

Schultz, D. P., & Schultz, S. E. (2015). *A history of modern psychology* (11th ed.). Wadsworth Publishing.

Seligman, M. E. P. (1999). The president's address. *American Psychologist, 54,* 599–562.

Seligman, M. E. P. (2004). *Authentic happiness: Using the new positive psychology to realize your potential for lasting fulfillment* (Reprint). Atria Books.

Seligman, M. E. P., & Csikszentmihalyi, M. (2000). Positive psychology: An introduction. *American Psychologist, 55*(1), 5–14. https://doi.org/10.1037/0003-066x.55.1.5

Seligman, M. E. P., Steen, T. A., Park, N., & Peterson, C. (2005). Positive psychology progress: Empirical validation of interventions. *American Psychologist, 60*(5), 410–421. https://doi.org/10.1037/0003-066x.60.5.410

Sinclair, S., Raffin-Bouchal, S., Venturato, L., Mijovic-Kondejewski, J., & Smith-MacDonald, L. (2017). Compassion fatigue: A meta-narrative review of the healthcare literature. *International Journal of Nursing Studies*, 69, 9–24. https://doi.org/10.1016/j.ijnurstu.2017.01.003

Solms, M., & Turnbull, O. H. (2011). What is neuropsychoanalysis? *Neuropsychoanalysis*, 13(2), 133–145. https://doi.org/10.1080/15294145.2011.107 73670

Suler, J. (2004). The online disinhibition effect. *CyberPsychology & Behavior*, 7(3), 321–326. https://doi.org/10.1089/1094931041291295

Summers, J. K., & Vivian, D. N. (2018). Ecotherapy – a forgotten ecosystem service: A review. *Frontiers in Psychology*, 9. https://doi.org/10.3389/fpsyg. 2018.01389

Teicher, M. H. (2006). Neurobiological consequences of early stress and childhood maltreatment: Are results from human and animal studies comparable? *Annals of the New York Academy of Sciences*, 1071(1), 313–323. https://doi.org/10.1196/annals.1364.024

Treanor, C., Kouvonen, A., Lallukka, T., & Donnelly, M. (2020). What is the acceptability of computerized cognitive behavioural therapy (cCBT) for adults? An umbrella review (Preprint). *JMIR Mental Health*. https://doi.org/10.2196/23091

Treger, S., & Masciale, J. N. (2018). Domains of similarity and attraction in three types of relationships. *Interpersona: An International Journal on Personal Relationships*, 12(2), 254–266. https://doi.org/10.5964/ijpr.v12i2.321

Walker, K. L. A., Ray, D. C., & Lollar, S. (2021). Integrating humanistic counseling and ecotherapy. *Journal of Professional Counseling: Practice, Theory & Research*, 49(1), 5–20. https://doi.org/10.1080/15566382.2021.1949209

Wampold, B. E., & Imel, Z. E. (2015). *The great psychotherapy debate: The evidence for what makes psychotherapy work (counseling and psychotherapy: Investigating practice from Sc)* (2nd ed.). Routledge.

Weiner, D. (1992). Philippe Pinel's "memoir on madness" of December 11, 1794: A fundamental text of modern psychiatry. (1992). *American Journal of Psychiatry*, 149(6), 725–732. https://doi.org/10.1176/ajp.149.6.725

White, M. P., Alcock, I., Grellier, J., Wheeler, B. W., Hartig, T., Warber, S. L., . . . Fleming, L. E. (2019). Spending at least 120 minutes a week in nature is associated with good health and wellbeing. *Scientific Reports*, 9(1). https://doi.org/10.1038/s41598-019-44097-3

Xu, B., & Zhuang, Z. (2020). Survey on psychotherapy chatbots. *Concurrency and Computation: Practice and Experience, 34*(7). https://doi.org/10.1002/cpe.6170

Yamaoka, Y., & Bard, D. E. (2019). Positive parenting matters in the face of early adversity. *American Journal of Preventive Medicine, 56*(4), 530–539. https://doi.org/10.1016/j.amepre.2018.11.018

Yovell, Y., Solms, M., & Fotopoulou, A. (2015). The case for neuropsychoanalysis: Why a dialogue with neuroscience is necessary but not sufficient for psychoanalysis. *The International Journal of Psychoanalysis, 96*(6), 1515–1553. https://doi.org/10.1111/1745-8315.12332